To Candice,
Live life to the fullest!
Victory is yours!

THE CRY OF
A WOMAN'S HEART

Healing the Pain of the Past
Traveling the Road to Victorious Living

3-12-11

Rebecca Simmons

All Scripture quotations in this book are taken from the King James Bible, New International Version.

THE CRY OF A WOMAN'S HEART

The Cry Of A Woman's Heart

For speaking engagements, you may contact the author at:
New Life Speakers
C/O Diligence Publishing Company
41 Watchung Plaza, #239
Montclair, New Jersey 07042
Website: www.NewLifeSpeakers.com
(973) 680-8438

ISBN: 0-9727416-2-3

Printed in the United States

Contents

Dedications

This book is dedicated to all of the beautiful women out there, even those of you who have not yet realized that you are wonderfully and fearfully made.

This book is also dedicated to the good men out there who have stood beside a beautiful woman, loved a beautiful woman, prayed for a beautiful woman, fathered a beautiful woman, been born of a beautiful woman, been a friend to a beautiful woman, or married a beautiful woman.

This book is dedicated to my mother, my sisters, my daughters and my girl friends.

This book is dedicated to my husband, my brother, my father and my sons.

This book is dedicated to my Pastor
Bishop Donald Hilliard Jr.

And finally,

Lord, I dedicate this book back to you. Bless it and use it for your Glory. Amen

♥♥♥♥

Introduction

The Cry Of A Woman's Heart

*The Spirit of the Sovereign Lord is on me, because the
Lord has anointed me to preach the good news to the
poor. He has sent me to bind up the brokenhearted.*
Isaiah 61:1

This book is for you. No matter how old or
young you are, by this point in your life you have
already experienced something that was meant to
destroy you. Molestation, betrayal, addiction, abuse,
heartbreak, abandonment, and depression all come
to steal your joy and kill the plans that God has
already ordained for your life. And if the truth were
to be told, many of us are suffering as a result of the
experiences in our lives that have caused us pain.

The devil has tried to destroy you, but I have good news for you. God is not finished with you yet! There is a greater purpose for your life and the pain from your past is hindering you from walking into it. Hence this book is my assignment from God.

God has put it upon my heart to write this book because He wants to minister to the cry of your heart and He wants to guide you on the path to healing the pain of your past so that you can experience victorious living today.

There are so many of us who appear to have it all together, yet we are hurting and broken human beings. God sees this and He sees the tears of those of us who weep in the night. He knows the hurt and the anguish of His children. For you see, even Jesus wept *(John 11:35)*.

God ordained me to write this book because He wants to give hope to you who were broken in your childhoods, in your early adult lives, and even those of you who are in your later years experiencing pain and discouragement. He has led me to share my own experiences as a testimony to His goodness and His mercy. He has led me to pray for you because prayer helps when nothing else will.

Open your heart and let this book minister to those secret places that only you and God know about. God wants to heal your pain and take away your discouragement, and He will do it if you let Him. So, journey with me as God takes us down the road that leads to healing and victorious living.

Let Us Start With This Prayer

Lord God, I thank you for hearing the cry of my heart. I thank you for everyone that will be ministered to through the reading of this book. I pray that you will hear the individual cries of their hearts as they look to you for healing.

Guide us through these inspirations for healing the pain of our past so that we can experience victorious living today. Let not one of us give up on the journey. Help us to press on towards the higher calling that is in your son, Christ Jesus; the calling of living a life that has you as the focal point, the calling of being virtuous women, and the calling of being filled with the joy of the Holy Spirit.

Lord, help my sisters to press on in spite of how much the unveiling may hurt. Heal my sisters and deliver them from evil so that they can walk with their heads held high and their hearts filled with joy. I thank you for showing us the way to victorious living. In the name of Jesus I pray. Amen.

<u>A WORD FROM THE LORD</u>

I have a great plan for your life. Put your trust in me.
I know that sometimes it's tough to believe when
there's so much that has caused you pain in this
lifetime. But if you seek me with your whole heart,
you will find me. Follow me. I will direct your paths
and lead you down the path of healing so that you
can live the life of purpose that I have already
ordained for you.

♥ Chapter 1

The Secret Pain

"Do not let your heart be troubled. Trust in God.
John 14:1

Pretending To Be Happy

Many of us walk around day after day and to the world we seem to be fine. When in fact, the reality is that we are hurting so much that we are afraid to stop moving. We think that if we stop being so busy, the pain would probably kill us. So we go on. We go on being wives and mothers, doctors and lawyers, cashiers and secretaries, deacons and ministers. We go on pretending until we have convinced everyone around us that we're happy.

We work hard to keep our pain a secret, because ultimately we know that if people knew what we were hiding, they would probably think less of us. Let's face it. If we let people in on our secret pain, then that pain would become more of a reality and most of us couldn't handle that.

You're Not Alone

I was in church one Sunday, and there was an altar call for everyone who had an issue that they needed God's help with. My spirit cried out deep inside of me when I realized that I was not the only one in pain. So many of my brothers and sisters stood at the altar and in the aisles crying out to God to take away the pain. It breaks my heart to see that so many people are hurting.

As sad as it is, many of us have a secret pain that eats away at the very essence of who we are. If we were in a war, and we are, we would be classified as the walking wounded. Some of us are actually the walking dead. We have already died inside and we don't really know if we have much more to live for. But, there is a glimmer of hope that keeps us going. Most of us feel that if we just keep faking it, one day we'll make it and the pain will miraculously go away.

When Numbness Sets In

As a matter of fact, it's not so bad on some days. Some of us actually get to the place where there is no pain at all. The only problem with this state of being pain free is the numbness that takes the place of the pain and the complacency that comes with being convinced that things are not going to change anyway, so we might as well accept things the way they are. Some people have this numbness, while others just have emptiness inside. At this point, there is no pain or numbness, just sheer emptiness. This is a bad place to be.

The Good News

No matter what you've been through in this life that's causing you so much pain, I have some good news! The good news is that Jesus is the ultimate painkiller and new life giver. Your pain can be diminished and the numbness brought to life again. The emptiness can be filled with joy and life can be abundant. Yes, these are the promises of God. God says He came for the hurting and the poor (Isaiah 61:1). He came to bring life back to those who have died inside. He came so that we could have life and have life more abundantly (John 10:10). If you believe these promises and accept them for your own life, you are well on your way to being healed from your secret pain; whatever it is.

This book will not heal you, but the Word of God that is contained within these pages will. God said that His Word will not return to Him without accomplishing everything that He sent it to do *(Isaiah 55:11)*. And He has sent His Word to heal every area of your heart where there is pain. But you must stop trying to run from the pain and you have to stop trying to hide the pain. In order to be healed you must face the pain and cry out to God telling Him where it hurts. God can heal you. He can make your heart brand new. I dare you to open up your heart and let the healing begin.

My Prayer For You

Lord God, I thank you for my sister reading this book right now. I pray that you will begin to minister to the areas of her heart and the areas of her life where there is secret pain. Lord, give her the courage to face whatever it is that she needs to face in order to be free from this thing that has hindered her from walking into the fullness of life. I pray her healing right now even as she stands in agreement with me. Help her Lord. Heal her Lord, and set her free from the bondage of her secret pain. And we will give you the glory, the honor and the praise. In Jesus' name I pray. Amen.

A WORD FROM THE LORD

You have suffered with this thing long enough. Come. Receive your healing. I will dry your tears. I will take away your pain. I will give you unspeakable joy. I will give you peace.

♥ Chapter 2

Broken, Busted, And Disgusted

For I know the plans I have for you, declares the Lord, plans to prosper you and not to harm you, plans to give you hope and a future.
Jeremiah 29:11

A Personal Testimony

I recall a time in my life when I was broken, busted and disgusted.

I was thirty-three years old, a single mother of a seventeen-year-old girl who was pregnant, living from paycheck to paycheck, and having a hard time trying to stay positive in spite of all of this. I had a job, but I didn't have much else.

During this period in my life, I remember wondering if perhaps there was something more to life, something that I was missing.

Can You Relate?

You may be able to relate to this. Murphy's law may be at work in your life right now. Everything that could go wrong has gone wrong and you don't know where to turn. You have been broken – you've been broken by bad relationships, broken by your past, broken by lack of hope for your future. Your hopes are busted and you are, at this point, totally disgusted. There are times when you wonder if there is a better way. There may be other times when you think that this is as good as it gets. So many of us have been at this point and we don't know what to do when we get here.

A Way Out

I thank God that it was during this very difficult time that I found out that there is a better way. Jesus said that He is the way, the truth, and the life *(John 14:6)*. I was looking for a better way, and I found it, through a relationship with Jesus. That relationship revealed to me the truth about the way that I was living and Jesus changed my life and gave me a new life. I was able to make it through all of the hard times and as I write this, I am 43 years old and I have more joy than I ever imagined I would have. Hallelujah! Jesus has, indeed, given me a new life.

But it didn't come without a sacrifice and I didn't get to this point overnight. Even as a new Christian I remember times when I felt like I couldn't make it, but then I remembered to look unto the hills because that was where my help was coming from. I remembered to look up, because that was where I wanted to go...up.

When you are at the end of your rope, remember to look up and reach up to the Lord in prayer. He will hear you and answer you.

Remember To Look Up!

When you are feeling like you are at the end of your rope, always remember to look up. Just looking up will remind you that you have a choice. You can go down, or you can choose to strive for something more. As you reach upwards beyond your circumstances, remember that your dreams can become a reality.

You may be broken, busted and disgusted right now, but you don't have to stay that way. There is so much more to life. Just think of all of the people who are fulfilling their dreams every day. Then think of those people who will die without fulfilling any of their dreams. Now you have to choose. Which one will you be? Will you just lie there and let life beat you up? Or are you going to stand and fight to achieve what has already been laid out for you?

The dreams that you have for your life did not appear out of nowhere. Your dreams were actually assigned to you by God before you were even born. Let me take it a little further and say that your dreams are part of the reason that you were born.

God's Plan

It is God's plan for you to succeed. His plan is for you to prosper and to be in good health, mentally, financially, spiritually, and physically *(3 John 2)*. You were not born to be defeated. You were born to win! Don't let any more time pass by before you begin to take hold of the things that God has planned for you. There will be times when you get discouraged. But when you do, remember that God's plans are to prosper you and to give you a future, not to harm you. He wants to first give you hope and then a future *(Jeremiah 29:11)*.

You must realize that there is no good future without hope. And hope has to be backed up by faith, because it is impossible to please God if you don't have faith *(Hebrews 11:6)*.

Now faith is being sure of what we hope for and certain of what we do not see. (Hebrews 11:1)

No matter what it looks like, God wants you to get to the point where you can believe Him enough to put all of your trust and all of your faith in Him as you move with certainty towards the unseen things that you hope for.

Is that a glimmer of faith-filled hope that I see? Fantastic! Now that you have hope for your future, let us move on and see what else is in store for you.

My Prayer For You

Lord God, I thank you for my sister reading this right now. She has been broken, busted and disgusted and she is seeking your face for her healing. She has carried the burden of the circumstances in her life this far, but sometimes she feels like she has reached the end of her rope. I ask that you touch her right now and help her to look up. Help her to look towards heaven because we know that is where her help will come from.

Give her hope for her future and give her a heart to have faith in you. Then, prosper her Lord.

Give her good health and a mind to serve you. In Jesus' name I pray. Amen.

A WORD FROM THE LORD

Do not be discouraged. Have faith in me. I have great things planned for you. As you draw nearer to me, I will prosper you...in your health, your finances and your soul.

♥ Chapter 3

Who Broke You?

Jonathon son of Saul had a son who was lame in both feet. He was five years old...His nurse picked him up and fled, but as she hurried to leave, he fell and became crippled. His name was Mephibosheth.
2 Samuel 4:4

Like Mephibosheth, many of us were dropped at a young age and we have ended up crippled and broken. That's pretty sad, but the saddest part of it all is that most of us do not want to deal with the issues that broke us.

My daughter has a lot of little dolls. She has dolls of all shapes and sizes. Some of her dolls are made of cloth and cannot be torn apart. However, she has a lot of dolls that are plastic, and the arms, legs and heads come off. One day when she was three, she came to me with Barbie. She calls all of her dolls Barbie, and she said to me, "Mommy, somebody broke Barbie." I asked her, "Who broke Barbie?" She shrugged her little shoulders as if to say, "I don't know."

This conversation with my three-year old reminds me of the question that pops into my head when I'm ministering to a woman who is hurting. *"Who broke you? Who dropped you when you were a child, causing you to have this concussion or this limp, this handicap that prevents you from having a normal, happy, productive life?"* I know that if I asked some of these women that question, their first reaction would be to look at me and shrug their shoulders as if to say, "I don't know."

Who broke you? Who damaged you? Who dropped the ball on you? Who abandoned you? Who abused you? Who disappointed you? Who did it? If I were to persist with this barrage of questions, the mental block would begin to become dislodged and most of the women would have this pained expression on their faces as they remembered the events of their childhood that they have so carefully concealed. Their minds would be screaming, *"Oh no, I couldn't possibly tell you who broke me. I couldn't tell you about that. After all, it was probably my fault anyway. I am the one with the problems. I am the one who is messed up. It's me!"*

I can definitely relate to these women. I've been there and if you would have asked me, "Who broke you?" I would have shrugged my shoulders and continued to hide the truth.

Crippled From Childhood

Jonathan's son was dropped when he was five years old. This child was crippled most of his life and never could walk after he was dropped. Because the person who was supposed to be taking care of him dropped him, he was messed up for most of his life. He was considered to be a nobody until David invited him to sit at his table, the table of the King *(2 Samuel 9:7)*.

After that, Jonathan's son was able to hold his head up and feel like he was somebody. I would like to think that someone told him, "It's not your fault that you're crippled. You were not born that way. Somebody dropped you." That's what God is telling me to tell you today, "It's not your fault. You were not born that way. Somebody dropped you!"

If you were abandoned as a child, if you were physically, sexually, or emotionally abused, if you were the child of an alcoholic or drug addict, if you were neglected, you were dropped and you are not to blame! And, just like Jonathan's son, you have been crippled for most of your life. You have been limping your way through life and the worst part about it is that you have believed the lie that you are a nobody and that you don't deserve to live a better life. But, just like Jonathan's son, you have been invited to sit at the table of the King. Yes you, with your crippled self. God will not allow you to keep going through life messed up. He knows that you were dropped, but He wants to heal you of your limp and make you whole again. Come on. You're invited. Won't you come and sit at the table of the king? It is at God's table that you'll receive your healing.

A place has been reserved for you at the table of the King!

My Prayer For You

Lord God, my King. I thank you for inviting me to sit at your table. It was there where I dined on the bread of life and drank of your living water that I received my healing. It was only through your invitation that was extended to me to sit at your table that I realized that I am somebody. So right now, I stand in the gap for my sister who's reading this book right now.

She was dropped in her childhood. She was neglected, molested, abandoned or abused and it left her broken. She has been limping through life and she is ready to be healed. I ask that you heal her of the spirit of being a victim and that you allow her to see that she is no longer a victim, but that she is more than a conqueror. She is indeed victorious. I ask that you heal her mind, her body and her spirit. I thank you right now for helping her to know that she is somebody in your eyes and I thank you for healing her brokenness. In Jesus' name I pray. Amen.

A WORD FROM THE LORD

I am the Lord your God. I will never leave you or forsake you. It is time for you to be whole again. Cast the load that has been crippling you on me. I will carry it for you. Trust me for I am the Lord your God.

♥ Chapter 4

The Truth About Drugs And Alcohol

Do not get drunk on wine, which leads to debauchery.
Instead, be filled with the Spirit.
Ephesians 5:18

This is the truth about drugs and alcohol – plain and simple, drugs and alcohol won't help. Oh it may seem like they are helping when you are under their influence. But guess what? You have to sober up some time and each time you wake up sober, the reality of what you were running from will hit you like a ton of bricks and you'll feel worse.

A Personal Testimony

I remember when I was so depressed and so disappointed with life that I just wanted to drink and do drugs. I would stay sober during the day so that I could go to work and then in the evening, I would have a drink or smoke some marijuana. These things put me into a fog so that I didn't have to think about my reality.

I Neglected My Daughter

Partying was my life. In the meantime, I had a teenage daughter who was crying out for my attention. But I couldn't help her because I was all messed up. I couldn't even help myself. When I sobered up, I still couldn't see her needs. All I saw were my needs and my problems so I reached for another drink or some more drugs. Eventually, my sweet little daughter found someone to listen to her needs. She found comfort in the arms of a young man who was five years older than she was. He understood all about her troubles and she fell head over heals in love with him.

Before I knew it, they were telling me that I was going to be a grandmother. You might think that this news would have sobered me up, but it didn't. I made up my mind that I wasn't going to deal with my daughter having a baby, I was going to keep tripping and keep getting high. At that point, the more I partied, the better. Needless to say, it didn't help.

Bad Relationships

I had a relationship at this time, but that wasn't working out. Neither had any other relationship that I had ever had. There was something wrong with me. I knew that much. Yes, I had been dropped and I was broken. I was trying to fix myself or at least, put some anesthesia into my system so that I couldn't feel the pain. Every time I sobered up, the painful memories tried to surface. I didn't want to deal with the pain from my past. I only wanted it to go away. So I picked up some liquor to ease the pain. Then I took it a little further, and I picked up a joint and some cocaine.

I remember one night during this time while I was dating this young man and we were having problems. I went to the liquor store and bought a bottle of this orange flavored liquor. God is so good that I don't even remember the name of it. But I took that bottle home and had some drugs and I consumed the whole bottle and did the drugs until I knocked myself out.

I woke up the next morning next to an empty bottle and an ashtray. I had a very bad headache and I felt horrible. I remember crying my eyes out because I felt so lost.

I Could Have Died

I went on like this for years. My looks were fading, I had no money so I could barely pay my rent or my bills, and I was very, very tired. When I think back, I realize that I could have died. I could have died from drinking and doing drugs and then driving while high. I could have been raped out there partying or worse yet, mugged and killed. I could have gotten AIDS. Although God spared my life from all of these consequences, I know that I was on the verge of dying. The truth about drinking and doing drugs is that these things didn't make me feel better. They actually made me feel worse. They were killing me! That is why I am telling you all of this. I have to testify that if life is getting you down and you need something to make you feel better, drugs and alcohol won't work. They only help to keep you crippled and broken until you are busted and disgusted.

The Problem, Not The Solution

I thank God that I am drug and alcohol free and have been for eight years. I believe that God let me go through that experience of using drugs and alcohol just to show me how miserable they could make me. He wanted to show me that the things of this world couldn't help me, that only He could ease my pain and heal my brokenness. He let me come out of that experience so that I could tell others to put down the bottle and put down the drugs and turn to Him through His son Jesus Christ. Drugs and alcohol are not the solution. They are actually part of the problem. You don't need them and if you were honest with yourself, you would admit that you feel worse after using them. Drugs and alcohol only make matters worse.

Generational Curses

Remember when we talked about being broken in the last chapter. If I can be totally open with you, I want to tell you that the person who broke you was probably a victim of those same drugs and alcohol that are tempting you. For instance, both of my parents drank alcohol. In my young eyes, my father was the best father in the world when he wasn't drinking. But when he got some alcohol in his system, things changed. Eventually, my parents broke up and my father moved out.

So you see, because my siblings and I lost our father, we all suffered as a result of our parents drinking. Two of my sisters have been battling with alcohol and drugs for years because of the influence of alcohol in our home when we were growing up.

Because of his drinking, my father dropped us and he crippled us. But his parents probably dropped him and crippled him too.

Stop The Cycle

We need to stop the cycle now. Not only for our own sakes but also for the sake of our children. The Bible says that the sins of the fathers will be visited upon the children to the third and fourth generation of those who hate God, but that the love of God will be shown to a thousand generations of those who love Him *(Deut. 5:9,10)*. If you are in a lifestyle of drugs and alcohol, you can't love God. You can't even love yourself. Therefore you are operating under this biblical curse. I am begging you. Don't let drugs and alcohol continue to wreck havoc in your life.

They may seem to be helping for a little while, but in the end they will destroy you and this cycle will be repeated in the lives of your children.

My Prayer For You

Lord God. I praise your holy name. I thank you for delivering me from the clutches of alcohol and drug use. I thank you for taking me out of the life of darkness and showering me with your marvelous light. I pray right now that you will bless my sister as she is reading this prayer right now. I pray that you will guide her and give her the strength to put down the bottle and the drugs. Help her to deal with the pain that led her to drink and do drugs in the first place. Help her to face her issues and to know that nothing is too big for you. Show her that she can bring all of her cares to you in prayer. I realize that my sister's problems may go back to when she was dropped as a child and I ask that you help her to deal with this thing that is driving her to drink and do drugs. Give her a safe harbor where she can go to talk to someone about her problems and where she can find understanding for her situation and direction for her life.

I thank you that you are taking the desire for the taste of alcohol and drugs from my sister right now. Give her a mind to seek after you to heal all of the issues of her heart. I thank you and I praise you. In Jesus' name I pray. Amen.

A WORD FROM THE LORD

I am the way, the truth and the life. Don't be discouraged when trials and tribulations come your way. Instead of turning to alcohol and drugs, turn to me. I have already made a way out for you. Seek my face and I will guide you through the challenging times in life.

♥ Chapter 5

A Ray Of Light In The Darkness

You are my lamp, O Lord; the Lord turns my darkness into light. – 2 Samuel 22:29

Molestation, Rape And Abuse

There was a beautiful young girl in the Bible named Tamar *(2 Samuel 13:1)*. She had a half brother who fell in love with her and began to lust after her. One day he pretended to be sick and tricked her into coming to his room to give him food. Once there, he grabbed her and raped her. She begged him to stop, but consumed by his demon of lust, he carried out his evil plan. When he was done with her, he became disgusted with her and had her thrown out of the house. She begged him not to cast her out but at that point, he was probably so consumed with guilt that he could no longer stand the sight of her.

This incident put Tamar in a very dark place. Not only did her brother rape her, but he also rejected her and cast her out. Heartbroken, she tore her beautiful robes and put ashes on her face.

These actions symbolize many things. The beautiful garments that were once a symbol of her virginity only served to remind her that she was spoiled goods and that since she was no longer a virgin, no man would ever take her for his wife. The tearing of the beautiful garments not only showed that she wasn't a virgin anymore, but this action, along with the ashes on her face, was also an expression of her anguish that this thing had happened to her. These actions also showed that she wasn't feeling beautiful anymore, and that she was now grieving the loss of her innocence and the loss of trust. I'm sure that she also mourned the loss of the relationship that she had with her brother before he raped her. This woman was violated and rejected by someone that she trusted.

Unfortunately, there are many of us today who have also been violated and rejected by men that we trusted. And often, the violation is in the form of incest and molestation. Then there are others of us who have been beaten or are still being beaten by men that we trusted. Finally, there's the woman who has been brutally raped and then tossed to the side like trash. All of these experiences are enough to make a woman feel ugly and undesirable. Being violated as a child or as an adult woman has a lasting impact.

The Secret Shame

As quiet as it is kept, one woman out of every three women was molested when she was a little girl. That's what the statistics say. But I am here to argue that the number of women who have experienced this horrible ordeal is much, much higher. The statistics of 1 out of every 3 only represents the number of woman that tell.

Tamar, the girl in the Bible story was told by her brother to be quiet. Her other brother, Absalom, instructed her not to tell anyone what had happened and she never told anyone. Her father found out about it, but he ignored what had happened and never did anything about it.

This happens far too often in the lives of victims of molestation today. It is usually the person who is molesting the girl that tells her not to tell. The girl is often told that it's 'their little secret' or even threatened that if she tells anyone that she will be hurt. One person even told me that her father told her that her mother would die of a heart attack if she told.

Misplaced Anger

Then, there are the brave young girls who dare to tell their mothers that their father, brother, stepfather, uncle or teacher is touching them or doing nasty things to them. These young girls are often in for a big shock when their mothers are not angry with the men, but their mothers are actually angry with them. Some of them are called liars, sluts, whores, and dirty. Then they are told to never say anything like that again.

So, much like Tamar, the girl has to go around feeling ugly and rejected. She has to deal with the guilt of feeling like it was her fault that this terrible thing has happened to her. She also has to bear the secret and the shame of having been violated or being continually violated. Finally, she has to deal with the pain from the realization that her mother, whom she also trusted to take care of her, is angry with her because of what happened. What's wrong with this picture? Why would a little girl have to take the blame for some pervert with a sexual disease using her for his own sick satisfaction?

I'm Mad As Hell!

If I sound upset, it's because I am. I have met and talked with too many women who have gone through this ordeal and spent the rest of their lives feeling ugly, dirty, worthless, and rejected. Because of this experience the women have not been able to have successful lives or relationships. To bury the pain, most of them turn to drinking, drugs, sleeping with every man that shows an interest in them, go-go dancing, prostitution, and homosexuality, Most of them have blocked out what happened to them and are trying to make it through life in spite of this nagging pain that they just can't explain. And because of the reaction from their mothers, these women do not dare tell anyone what happened to them when they were children. What would people think? Would they blame these women for being sexually abused by the men that they trusted to protect them? Would they? Would you?

It's time to take a good look at the issue of molestation. We need to be educated about this issue and aggressive enough to speak out against this demon that is destroying young lives every day.

Unmasking The Issue Of Child Molestation

It's time for us to take the veil off of the issue of molestation of minor children I say children because little boys are being molested too, and this is definitely rarely talked about. Mother, if your child tells you that he or she is being touched or made to do sexual things, you must take the time to investigate what they are telling you. Chances are that the child is telling you the truth. There are many children being molested today. Don't let your child be one of them, and if it is happening in your home and the child tells you about it, get the accused person out of your house and keep them out! Also, if the person denies it – and they will – it is still your duty to your child to protect her or him from the person until you have all of the facts. Take the child to the doctor and a psychologist. Forget your own embarrassment. Forget your shame and see about your child.

If You Were Molested

Now I want to talk to those of you who have been molested. Chances are you are one of the ones who didn't tell. You have been carrying this dirty, dark secret around for so long that you don't even recognize the pain anymore. And if you do feel a twinge of that old familiar ache, you hurry up to find something to medicate yourself with.

You've been in one bad relationship after another, and you have done some things that you are ashamed of. Your relationships never work out because any time a man gets too close to you, you push him away. You make sure that you pick men who are emotionally or somehow unavailable to you just to be on the safe side. After all, you don't want to fall in love with Mister Right only to have him reject you. Even if you're married, you're probably having problems making love with your husband because subconsciously, you feel dirty and you feel that sex is dirty.

Married or single, the truth of the matter is that you just don't trust men. And besides that, you don't even think you're worthy of having a good man to love you.

Well, my sister. I've been sent to tell you that you have been carrying the burden of guilt and shame for too long. The shame and guilt were never yours to carry in the first place. Yes, you were molested. Yes, you were raped. You may even have been blamed for what happened. But you don't have to be ashamed about it and you don't have anything to be guilty about. You didn't do anything wrong! What happened to you was not your fault! There was nothing that you could have done to prevent it from happening. You didn't make them do it. You are not to blame for someone imposing his or her sick will on you. It was not your fault. So hold up your head, my sister, because yes, you are still that beautiful girl from so very long ago. Don't you know that you are fearfully and wonderfully made? You are awesome to behold. Yes, I'm talking about you. You do deserve to be happy. You do deserve a good man in your life. You do deserve the blessings that the Lord has in store for you.

If You Were Raped

And for you, my sister, yes you, the one who was gang raped by that group of boys at that college campus fraternity party. And the one who was snatched into an alleyway on the way home one night, and you, the one who was forced to have sex with the guy who you were on a date with even though you told him no; the same thing goes for you. It was not your fault. It's never your fault when someone forces you to have sex. No matter where you were, what you were wearing, or what you may have been doing before the actual rape, no means no! So you have to realize that although you were forced to bear the burden of this awful thing that happened to you, you are not to blame. It wasn't your fault! You never asked to be touched or to be raped. You didn't make them do it. You were a victim.

No Longer A Victim

But you don't have to live the rest your life as a victim. By breaking the silence, you will feel the chains that have kept you in bondage for so long drop from you and hit the floor. If you have been a victim of sexual abuse or of rape, find someone that you can talk to and confide in them about what happened. For some of you, that may be your husband or your best friend. For others, that person may be your Pastor or a counselor. For others, there are support groups where you can go to meetings or interact with others online. Whatever you do, don't let that thing continue to eat you up on the inside and destroy your life.

End The Cycle Of Abuse

Finally, I would like to talk to the woman who is in an abusive relationship right now. If you grew up under abusive conditions, if you were raped or molested, or even if you saw your father beating your mother, chances are that you will at some point end up in a relationship where you will have to choose between fighting back or getting the stew beat out of you, or you may display aggressive behaviors in your relationships with men.

A Personal Testimony About Violence

My mother and father used to argue and fight a lot when I was a kid. I never realized how much of an impact hearing them fight had on my life until I realized that I was a violent person. I would actually pick fights with the men in my life. In my twisted mind, I believed that if I could provoke them to get angry enough to hit me, then that meant that they really cared about me. I think I had at least one fight with each and every man that I had a relationship with.

This cycle ended when I was dating my husband. He told me in no uncertain terms that he wasn't like the rest of the men that I had dealt with in my life. He flat out refused to put his hands on me. This literally blew my mind, but it also opened my eyes to show me that I had the wrong understanding of what love is. I thank God for that man and the stand that he took in refusing to fight me.

Love Is Never Violent

If you have to fight someone to prove that they love you, you have learned the wrong lesson about love. Love is kind, gentle and caring. Love is not violent. I repeat. Love is never violent.

On the other hand, you may not be as crazy as I was. You may be absolutely innocent, but some man is taking the liberty to beat you up whenever he gets angry about something, or whenever he gets drunk. I advise you to run. Don't walk, but run away from him as fast as you can. If he is to the point of threatening to kill you, then you need to be careful about how you leave. It is best for you to contact an agency that helps battered women. They will advise you on the best way to get out and stay out. I do know that it's important that you don't go someplace where you can easily be found. When you do get out, make it a point to stay away from him. Don't look back! Don't go back! Don't even have a telephone conversation with him unless he can find a way to prove to you that he has quit drinking and gotten help for his anger problem.

Leave The First Time He Hits You

Abuse is a dangerous thing and women are getting killed everyday at the hands of the men that they love. Being punched and kicked around is not love. The key to avoiding the worst-case scenario is to leave him the very first time that he puts his hands on you in an aggressive manner. If he will shove you or hit you once, he'll shove and hit you again and again and again. Each time it will get worse. So don't play with fire. Set the standard from the very beginning.

If you have to fight to be with someone, it's not worth it. It's just not worth it. And don't ever let anyone tell you that you made him hit you. Under no circumstances should a man ever hit a woman. Period! You were not created to be some man's punching bag. You were created for God's pleasure. He delights in seeing you happy, not bruised and battered.

Breaking The Bondage Of Shame

All of the above scenarios remind me of Tamar's situation. Being sexually abused, raped and battered all leave us with a sense of helplessness and an even greater sense of shame. We end up living in the shadows of life, afraid that someone is going to find out that we've been molested, raped or abused or that we're being beat up on a regular basis.

It's time to be loosed from this bondage. You can never live up to your full potential as long as you are bowed down under the burden of all of that baggage. So it's time to unpack your bags and leave them right at the altar with Jesus.

Jesus Is The Light Of The World

Jesus is the ray of light in the darkness. He came to be a light to the world. He came to shine the light on your life so that you could see the areas that need to be healed. His light will take you out of the darkness of mourning. His light will take you out of the darkness of despair. His light will guide you as you continue on the path of victorious living.

The Bible tells us to give God our worries and our cares because He cares about us *(I Peter 5:7)*. He promises to heal the broken heart and to replace your tears with joy *(Isaiah 61)*. If we really believe the Word of God, we've got to believe that God changes lives. We've got to believe that nothing is impossible with God and we've got to believe that God cares about us, and that with Him on our side, there is no more shame and there is no more guilt *(Romans 8:1)*. There is only the grace of God, which restores our souls and fills our hearts with joy overflowing.

Let Us Pray Together

Lord God, I thank you for your wonderful, healing Word. I thank you for your son, Jesus, who you sent to be a light to the world. I thank you that He makes the light to shine in the dark areas of our lives that we would rather keep hidden.

I thank you for not allowing us to live in darkness anymore. Lord God, I present to you my sister. She has been abused, molested, raped or battered. Lord, she has been a victim of life's circumstances and it has left her hurting, bruised, scared, empty, frustrated, angry, bitter, and feeling worthless. She has put the ashes on her head and ripped away any remaining beauty believing that no one would want her after such an experience. Lord, I ask that you speak to her heart right now and tell her that none of this was her fault. Tell her that she is worth something. Tell her that she is worth far more than rubies.

Lord God, I ask that you comfort her while she deals with the pain of her trauma. Heal her totally of all of the emotions that she experiences as a result of what happened. Help her to forgive those who hurt her and those who failed to protect her. Help the victim of molestation or rape to forgive herself for all of the behavior that she displayed over the years while she was trying to deal with this thing on her own. Help the battered woman who's still in an abusive relationship to get out and stay out. Help her to know that she deserves better than to be beaten up by someone. Now Lord God, I pray for total healing for my sister right now. Restore her beauty and restore everything that the enemy took away from her. I pray that she will be a strong tower to help others who have had to endure this same experience.

Deliver her from shame and deliver her from guilt. Free her from the power of the enemy over her mind that would have her to continue to believe that she did something to deserve such treatment. I pray for fullness of joy to be returned to her. In the matchless name of Jesus I pray. Amen.

A WORD FROM THE LORD

Lift up your head my daughter. I died to set you free from the shame and the guilt of your past. I will turn those things that the enemy planned for your destruction into power for my Kingdom. Leave the past behind and step forward into the destiny of joy, peace and abundance that I have already prepared for you.

♥ Chapter 6

Learning To Forgive

Get rid of all bitterness, rage and anger, brawling and slander, along with every form of malice. Be kind to one another, forgiving each other, just as in Christ God forgave you. – Ephesians 4:31-32

Unresolved Anger

If you were molested, neglected, abused, or raped, or if you have been hurt over and over again in your life, you probably have some unresolved anger in your heart.

Unresolved anger can make you fell like hurting someone or even killing somebody. I am not amazed that every time I pick up the paper or turn on the news, there are stories about people that are getting so angry that they are actually committing murder. I would adamantly argue that these people's anger did not start with the people that they killed, but that the anger had been in their hearts for a long time. I'm talking about unresolved anger. Unresolved anger is anger that has not been dealt with, anger that has not been forgiven and, as you can see by our headlines and news reports, if left unchecked, unresolved anger is deadly.

Violence

A lot of the violence that we see in our headlines is the result of unresolved anger. A lot of violence that we see in our homes is the result of unresolved anger. This violence can be resolved by one simple act, the act of forgiveness. "Now wait a minute," you might say, "Forgiveness is not simple. You don't know what that person did to me!" I agree. But I would like to offer that forgiving those who have hurt you is much simpler than living with the burden of carrying that anger around in your heart and having it do much more harm to you than what that person did to you.

Sickness And Destructive Behaviors

Not only does unresolved anger invoke violence, but it also causes sicknesses like high blood pressure, diabetes, arthritis, stress, cancer and heart disease. Unresolved anger also leads to behaviors like alcoholism and drug abuse.

A Personal Testimony About Anger

For many years, I carried unresolved anger in my heart. I was angry with my father, my mother, my first husband and everyone else who had hurt me in my life. Each new hurt added another layer to the ugly scab that anger was forming on the inside of me. It got to the point where I would lash out at the least little thing. I was a total mess and I couldn't figure out why it took so little to set me off. Then one day, I heard about one simple act – the act of forgiveness. I heard that Jesus had died on the cross so that I could be forgiven for my sins. I heard that God sent Jesus to die for me because He loved me. I realized that Jesus must have loved me too because He put His life on the line for me. This one simple act has changed my life. It has also taught me how to forgive others.

Who Am I Not To Forgive?

After receiving such forgiveness from God for all that I had done wrong in my life, who am I not to forgive those who have hurt me over the years? So I made up my mind to forgive everyone that had hurt me and I did. I forgave my father, my mother and my ex-husband. I forgave the person that molested me. I even forgave my cousin who had slept with my boyfriend when I was eighteen. I forgave them all. As life goes on, I find that I'm still forgiving people today.

You're Only Hurting Yourself

In order to have the abundant life that God has planned for you, you have to forgive those people who have hurt you. Chances are it won't be easy to do because the first instinct is to stay angry with people and make them pay for hurting you. Well, my sister, I have news for you. When you stay angry with someone, you are not hurting that person. The truth of the matter is you are only hurting yourself. Holding a grudge will make you miserable and sick. Anger can and will kill you.

Besides in most cases the person that hurt you will not even be affected by your anger. They've already gone on with their life, but you are the one who's suffering. Unwillingness to forgive destroys your mind, your body and your spirit. Your relationships with everyone else will also be affected if you refuse to forgive those who hurt you in the past as well as those who will hurt you as you go through life. It may help to know that as long as you live, there's going to be someone around that will hurt you or let you down, but God will never harm you, nor will He allow you to be hurt beyond that which you can stand *(I Corinthians 10:13)*. However, God will allow you to experience some pain in your life. This is only so that you can see the areas in your life that need to be submitted to His will.

God's Plans Are Better Than Our Plans

If we believe that God has our best interests at heart and that His plans are better than our plans, we will be able to better handle it when someone hurts or disappoints us. We will be able to see beyond that person and see that it all fits into the perfect plan that God has for our lives. His Word says that He wants to prosper us (to make us better and give us peace as well as increase) and not to harm us *(Jeremiah 29:11)*. His Word also says that if you don't forgive someone, than God won't forgive you of your trespasses *(Matthew 6:15)*. He instructs us to forgive those who have hurt us *(Mark 11:25)*.

I want to encourage you to get with God's program and forgive someone today. You'll release them, but more importantly than that, you'll be setting yourself free. Un-forgiveness hinders you from reaching your God-given destiny. You want to always keep a forgiving heart so that you'll be able to move forward towards the greater calling that God has ordained for your life.

But one thing I do; Forgetting what is behind and straining toward what is ahead, I press on toward the goal to win the prize for which God has called me heavenward in Christ Jesus. (Philippians 3:13-14)

My Prayer For You

Lord God, I thank you for helping me to forgive those who have hurt me in the past. I thank you for creating in me a pure heart that's willing to forgive those who trespass against me almost daily.

I pray that you will grant this same grace to my sister who is reading this right now. I pray that you will help her to search her heart to identify the hurts that have not yet been forgiven. And then I ask that you will help her to forgive the people who created those hurts. I ask that you will give her the power to release the hatred, the resentment and the bitterness that she has been harboring against those who have caused her pain. I ask that you will give her peace and joy that comes from allowing you to avenge those who persecute her.

Lord God, help my sister right now to get free from the bondage of un-forgiveness and begin to heal her of the backache, the arthritis, the diabetes, the cancer, the stress, or any other sickness that she has been dealing with. We know that anger and un-forgiveness is a poison, so cleanse her of this poison and heal her body of the side affects of the anger that she has carried around for so long. Lord, help my sister to not only forgive those who have hurt her, but help her to forgive herself for all of the wrong thoughts and actions in her life.

Help her to receive your forgiveness. Help her to know that your son, Jesus, was born, lived and died so that she could be forgiven by you. And once she receives your forgiveness, help her to forgive herself and to forgive others. Then, help her to release her anger and not to pick it back up. Give her the grace to walk in the spirit and not the flesh in all that she does in life. For this, I will continually give you the glory, the honor, and the praise. In the name of Jesus I pray Amen.

A WORD FROM THE LORD

Un-forgiveness has hindered you from the great
things that I have planned for you to do. Release
those who have hurt you by forgiving them just as I
have forgiven you. Vengeance is mine. I will judge
those who come against you and harm you. Do not
be concerned with evildoers. Although it looks like
they are getting away with murder, in the end, if they
don't turn from their wicked ways, they will perish.

♥ **Chapter 7**

Looking For Love
In All The Wrong Places

I will get up now and go about the city. Through its
streets and squares I will search for the one my heart
loves. So I looked for him but did not find him.
Song of Songs 3:2

What's Love?

Love. What's it all about anyway? Do we even
know what love is? I'm sure that most of us would
admit that we have spent a big part of our lives
looking for love. For many years, I was out there
looking for my true love. I had this idea that true love
was like the fairy tales that I had read as a little girl.
You know the ones: Cinderella, Snow White and the
Seven Dwarfs, and Rapunzel.

Or how about the princess who kissed the frog
who was really a prince? Speaking of princes, there

was always the prince who would come in and save the girl from her dreadful conditions. Cinderella had a wicked stepmother, with Snow White, it was the wicked witch, and Rapunzel was locked up in a tower by a mean old woman. But in the end, they were all swept off of their feet by the tall, good-looking Prince Charming.

I used to love these fairy tales and dreamed of the day when my knight in shining armor would come and take me away, riding me off into the sunset on his beautiful white stallion.

From Fairy Tale Love To Soap Opera Drama

As I grew into puberty, the fairy tales were replaced by the soap operas that my mother was always watching when I came home from school. I would plop down on the couch and join her as she watched one soap opera star after another deceive her husband, sleep with her sister's boyfriend, lie to her lover, and get slapped around by her man or the woman that she had betrayed. At the end of each episode, she would end up somewhere crying and miserable.

The same thing was going on in the nighttime soaps that my mother watched. It seemed that everyone on these shows was lying, cheating, sleeping with somebody else's husband or boyfriend and getting slapped around. And there was always the bottle of booze or the prescription drugs to take away the pain.

Real Love?

In my immature mind, I reasoned that this was real love. I mean the fairy tales were one thing, but I didn't know anyone with a fairy tale romance. Everyone that I knew was doing what these people were doing in the soap operas. Even my own parents had issues and most of my friends didn't have a father in the home.

By the time my father moved out when I was ten, I was convinced that what was being portrayed on the soap operas was real love. I no longer dreamed about Prince Charming coming to take me away on his beautiful white horse. Now I dreamed that I was being cheated on and lied to by my boyfriend. Notice that I said boyfriend and not husband, because now that I think about it, most of these people on the soap operas were not even married. The women were just going from man to man and bed to bed. Does this sound familiar? It does to me. By the time I was in my early teens, I was already taking love anywhere that I could get it.

From Low Self Esteem To No Self Esteem

There was a nineteen-year-old boy who lived in my apartment building and he started paying attention to me. Since I didn't have a father around to affirm me, I developed the biggest crush on this boy. I saw his attention as an affirmation that I was pretty. You see I had always been very shy because I thought that I was ugly.

When my father dropped me, not only was I hurt, but it also left me with a limp of low self-esteem. I used this older boy's attention as a bandage for the wounds that were still giving me so much pain. Eventually, he convinced me to have sex with him. After taking my virginity, this boy tried to set me up for his friends to pull a sex train on me.

Can you imagine me as a young girl having just lost her virginity to this older boy that I'm crazy about and he sends his brother and his friends in for them to have sex with me? Well, I thank God that even then I was blessed with the gift of talking myself out of any situation and I was able to talk the boys into letting me go without anyone else touching me.

But at that point my low self-esteem had plummeted all the way down to no self-esteem. I was on a fast track to trouble with no brakes.

Love On The Rebound

To soothe the pain of what this boy had done to me, I immediately found myself another boyfriend. This one was seventeen going on eighteen. I was still fourteen and I fell head over heals in love with this young man, giving him my heart, soul and body so that he could validate me. Eventually, he left to go to the army. He wrote me letters telling me how much he loved me and that we were going to get married when I turned eighteen. Well, don't you know that he had not been gone six months when I heard from his sister that he had gotten married in Germany and that his wife was expecting a baby?

Fifteen Years Old And Pregnant – Now What?

Devastated, I cried on my friend Jimmy's shoulder. Jimmy said that I should be his girl. So I became his girl and together, we decided to have a baby. I was pregnant at fifteen. I became a mother at sixteen, dropped out of school and went on welfare. My baby's daddy went to jail for breaking and entering. So what does a girl with no self-esteem do now? Well, I just went right on in the direction that I had been going – nowhere fast. That's when I first started smoking marijuana and drinking beer. Then I went out and found another boyfriend.

Drama, Drama And More Drama

Just like the soap operas, my relationships were always full of drama. I remember when I was eighteen and my cousin came up from Florida for the summer. Before the summer was over, she had sex with my boyfriend. I broke up with him and moved on to the next boyfriend.

This cycle repeated itself over and over again from my teenage years to my early thirties. Every time the boy or man in my life messed up, I replaced him with another boy or man. Does this sound familiar?

I Was A Fool For Love

Then I started getting tired of going from man to man. So, I figured that I would settle down. I wanted a longer-lasting relationship. So, I ended up taking mess from men that I never took before. I found myself in relationships that were obviously doomed for failure from the start. I remember being in a relationship with a guy who told me that he would not commit to me. Does this sound familiar?

He told me that he would always have female friends and he even told me that he would marry me and take me to Africa. There I would help him to pick out his second wife. Can you believe that I stayed with him for at least another year even after he told me all of this? And to make matters worse, he said that he wasn't going to marry me unless I got pregnant. He wanted me to prove to him that I could still have babies. I thank God that I wasn't foolish enough to get pregnant by this guy.

What's The Deal Ladies?

I just have one question: What's the deal ladies? Men are still running these tired lines down to us and we are still falling for them. There is always going to be the married man who tells you that he and his wife are only staying together for the kids. He doesn't love her anymore, he tells you. As a matter of fact, they don't even sleep together. He sleeps on the couch, the floor, in the basement, in the garage, in another bedroom, or perhaps even the bathtub. Come on. Give me a break!

Then there's the man who's been with his girlfriend for over five years and together they own a house and cars, and they have a joint bank account. He claims that she won't leave even though she knows that he's not happy and that he's cheating on her. So he comes to you wining and dining you and telling you that you are the one who makes him happy. But he still goes back home to her every night. What's up with that? And, so what if you talk him into spending the night or the weekend? When he's done using your body for his pleasure, he's still going home to her.

Oh, and how about the man that pretends that you are the only one, but you find phone numbers in his pocket and there are two less condoms in his bedside drawer then there were the last time you were at his house? What's up with that?

More Foolishness On My Part

Let me tell you, I once went to a boyfriend's house unexpectedly and found a used condom on the floor in the guest room. There was a towel on the floor and when I picked up the towel, it dropped out. When I confronted him about it, he told me that he had used the condom to masturbate.

Can you believe that? Well, I didn't. As hard as I tried and as much as I wanted to, I couldn't believe such a story. Needless to say, that was the beginning of the end of our relationship, but do you know that it still took me several months to finally break up with this guy?

Why Do We Do The Things We Do?

Why do we do that? Why do we put up with the lies and the infidelities and the refusal from our men to commit to us in a one on one relationship? Why do we give our bodies and our souls to these men, have babies for these men, and cook and clean for these men when they refuse to marry us?

I would like to offer that it is possibly because we have been dropped, abused, abandoned, or ignored by our fathers and we are looking for someone to validate us. We are looking for someone to make us feel better. We are, indeed, looking for love in all of the wrong places.

Stop The Madness!

My sister, it's time to stop the madness! We need to open our eyes and take a good look at our relationships. We need to take a good look at the men that we allow to occupy space in our lives. And then we need to take a good look at the girl in the mirror. While you're looking at her, ask her why she allows herself to be used, abused, neglected, cheated on and lied to. Ask her why she has been lying to herself and making herself believe that all she wants in her relationships is sex. Ask her why she is denying the fact that deep down inside, she yearns to be loved by and married to that special someone who will treat her like a queen. Now, don't rush that girl in the mirror. Give her some time to answer you.

Listening To The Girl In The Mirror

What did she say? Are those tears in her eyes? Did she tell you how much she misses her father? Did she tell you how angry she is at him for leaving her? Did she tell you how that person hurt her when they touched her down there when she was a little girl? Did she tell you how afraid she was when her father beat her mother? Did she tell you how hurt she was when her mother beat her and called her names like stupid and ugly? Did she tell you that if her father didn't want her that every other man who sees her will? Did she tell you the secrets of her heart that you keep making her keep inside? Did she tell you? Did she tell you? Did she?

Facing The Pain

My sister if you will take that look into the mirror of your heart and allow yourself to face the pain that's inside, you will be on your way to a real healing; The kind of healing that no man can give you. I'm asking you to open up your heart and let God do the surgery.

Let God Validate You

I was a young girl, abandoned by my father, molested by someone that I trusted. I looked to men all of my life to make me feel like I was somebody. I also used sex, alcohol and drugs to make myself feel better.

Although I put on a good front and acted like I was all of that and a bag of chips, inside I felt like I was insignificant. And I allowed myself to be treated like I was insignificant in my relationships. Yes, my sister, I was looking for love in all of the wrong places.

But one day I heard that God knew me before I was born. I heard that He had carefully formed me in my mother's womb. I heard that He knew exactly how I would look and He even knew how many hairs I would have on my head. I heard that He knew the path that I would take. I heard that He had always been with me, through it all. I heard that He had seen my behavior over the years.

God Knows All About You

Oh yes. God has watched my every step and He has watched your every step. He knew what you were going to do before you did it. He knows about that married man. He knows about that homosexual encounter. He knows about the time you had more than one sex partner at a time. He knows about the drug-filled nights and the one night stands. God knows all about you and He knows all about me. This frightened me at first, when I thought about all of the things that I had done.

He Loves You In Spite Of What You've Done

But the best thing that I heard is that God loves me. He loves me in spite of what I've done. He loves me in spite of what I've been through. He cares about me. As a matter of fact, I heard that He has a plan for my life. He sent His son Jesus to die for me so that I could have life. Jesus died so that I could be forgiven by God the Father for my sins. He died so that I could have a chance to live. Not the way that I had been living, but so that I could have a good life filled with good things and that includes good relationships.

So, I'm here to share with you what I heard. My sister, you must come into the realization that God loves you in spite of what you've done. You must know that He really does want only the best for you. You have to know that His forgiveness is available to you. He wants you to know that you don't have to live like that. You can have a better life, an abundant life if you will only believe and receive the promises of God for yourself.

God Sent A Man Into A Bar To Get Me

God cares so much about you that He had me write this book so that you can read about His love. He cared so much about me that He sent a man into a bar in Newark, New Jersey to tell me about His love. I'm serious. One night when I was out partying, I met this fine man named Anthony. We danced and had a good time and at the end of the night he said, "I'm so excited. We're having a men's conference at our church and my Pastor is going to be speaking to the men tomorrow."

I almost fell out. What was this dear, sweet church boy doing in the Vanity Club in Newark? He asked me to come to church several times over the next few weeks, and each time I turned him down. I told him that I was happy with my life just the way it was. And I actually believed what I was telling him. But I was curious about why his eyes were so bright and why his smile was so joyful, so I agreed to go with him to church.

The Unforgettable Experience

I walked into the Cathedral International, then the Second Baptist Church in Perth Amboy, New Jersey, and experienced what the members there call the 'unforgettable experience.' I must say that the experience was indeed unforgettable and ten years later, I'm still going back every week.

It was there at the Cathedral that I heard about God and His goodness and His mercy. It was there that I was saved, filled with the Holy Spirit and baptized. God healed me through the ministry at the Cathedral. I learned that I am fearfully and wonderfully made and that I am the top and not the bottom, the head and not the tail. I also learned that I am worthy of being loved. That revelation helped me to love myself.

Healed By Real Love

It was the love of God that healed me. The love of God is real love. I no longer have to run here and there looking for someone to love me. As a matter of fact, I now love myself more than I love any man and I love God more than anything.

In return for my love, God has given me a man that loves me more than any man has ever loved me. This man loves the real me, not the me that I used to pretend to be. He knows me and understands me and in spite of myself, he still loves me. Although my husband Anthony, yes the guy who I met at the club, adds immensely to my happiness, it is not his love that I depend upon to make me happy. The full measure of my happiness comes from deep inside of me. That's where the Spirit of God lives and it is this Spirit that gives me unspeakable joy.

My Prayer For You

Lord God. I thank you for my sister right now. I pray that you will help her to see what real love is. I thank you for the experiences that you have allowed me to go through. But I thank you even more that you kept me through them all. I thank you for sending your people to tell me about your love.

I pray right now that my sister is assured of your love for her. I ask you to help her to stop looking for love in all of the wrong places. I ask that you will release her from going from man to man and bed to bed. Also, that you will stop the cycle of failed relationships in her life. I pray that you will fill the void that was left in her heart when her father left her life. Whether it was before she was born, due to his death, or due to his just leaving, I pray for healing for my sister right now. Help her to accept you as her new Father.

Validate her right now Lord. Show her the magnitude of your love and concern for her as she reads the rest of this book. Heal her of the heartbreak that she has endured in her relationships so far. Clear her mind of the guilt of being with men that did not belong to her. Strip her of the spirit of any unclean and perverted sex act that she has engaged in. Forgive her for her loose style of living and give her a brand new start. I pray this in the precious name of Jesus Christ. Amen.

A WORD FROM THE LORD

You are so special to me. I love you so much that I gave my only son, Jesus Christ, to die so that you could have a better life. Bask in my love for you. I love you like no man on this earth can ever love you.

♥ Chapter 8

God Sees Your Tears

And God will wipe away every tear from their eyes.
Revelation 7:17

Have you ever been so distressed that you just cried and cried? Have you found yourself smiling when you go out in public, but when you're home you just sit in a corner and weep? As I shared in the section on drugs and alcohol, there was a period in my life when I was so sad that I had to stay high in order to forget about the things that were causing me so much pain.

Life In A Fog

For about eighteen years, I lived my life in a fog. I started smoking marijuana and drinking beer when I was fourteen. Then I moved on to liquor and cocaine by the time that I was eighteen. By the time I was twenty-five, I had experimented with mescaline but after a bad trip, decided that I'd stick with the booze, marijuana and cocaine. So for the next six years, I was a functional addict. It's funny because recently my sister who is a recovering addict asked me if I was an addict and I quickly said, "No." I told her that I just used drugs and drank alcohol every day but I wasn't an addict. But when I think about it, I think that I do fall into the category of having been a functional addict. I went to work everyday and functioned just fine, but every night, I needed to have a drink and smoke a joint or something. I was even free enough to reserve my cocaine usage to weekends because I didn't want to go to work with glassy eyes. But the bottom line is I needed this stuff to make it in life. And whether I like it or not, that qualified me as an addict.

Our God Is Merciful

I thank God that I never hit rock bottom. I thank Him that when I got sick and tired of depending on drugs to make life all right, I was able to stop without going to a rehabilitation program or meetings or anything like that. God was so merciful to me that I didn't even have to go through withdrawal when I stopped using drugs and drinking. Because I didn't think I was saved, (I had forgotten about the altar call for salvation that I took when I was nine years old) when I stopped using cocaine and smoking marijuana, I thought that I had stopped on my own strength.

The way it happened was strange. One day I was looking in the mirror and I looked into my eyes. I didn't like the way that my eyes looked so glassy and I made the decision at that moment to stop using drugs. And just like that, I stopped. I even had to stop going to my get high buddy's house because she would always have drugs around when I went there and I didn't want to be involved in that scene anymore. But I realize now that the hand of God was on my life even then. It was God's will that caused me to stop getting high. God was with me even though I didn't know it. He was taking care of me even when I was barely taking care of myself.

A Honeymoon Revelation

Two years later, I accepted God back into my life. For the next year and a half I was attending church on a regular basis but I was still having a drink or two whenever I felt like it. Which became less and less often, because all of a sudden, I was feeling better than I had felt in years. I had my last drink when we went on our honeymoon to Jamaica.

Now anyone who's been to this particular resort at Montego Bay knows that all they do there is party from the time they get up in the morning until they fall out. Well, Anthony and I jumped right in and started drinking Strawberry Daiquiris made with Jamaican rum at about 10:00 in the morning on our first day there (with our saved selves). Before noon, we were arguing. He looked at me and I looked at him and I said to him, "Let's not drink anymore while we're here. Okay?" He agreed and we drank Virgin Daiquiri's from that point on. We both realized that if we were going to make it as a married couple, we would have to stop drinking.

When we got home, the first thing that I did was open my liquor cabinet and pour out all of the wine and liquor that was in there. That was that, the end of my drinking days.

Reality Sinks In

As time went on and I stayed sober, reality started to sink in. I was forced to deal with the past pain that I had kept medicated by the drugs and booze for so long. In addition to that, I had to deal with the present pain of being married to a man that had a son who blatantly rejected having me in his life. I must tell you that I spent many nights crying because his rejection hurt so much. Then, to make matters worse, I felt like my husband didn't understand why I was so upset. I also felt like he was harboring feelings of resentment towards me whenever I complained to him about something that his children had done.

I was a newlywed, but I felt like my marriage was over before it could get off to a good start. Anthony and I were arguing all of the time, and I felt that I had somehow been bamboozled into thinking that I could be happily married. It got to the point where I had to fight daily against feelings of loneliness, hurt, anger, bitterness, resentment, and hopelessness. Because of the disappointment in my new marriage, I became bitter and that bitterness turned into resentment towards my husband and my new eight-year-old son. I was also angry with myself for letting myself get into such a mess. Before the wedding, I had been convinced that we were all going to be one big happy family. Such was not the case and I was ticked off about it.

The pain that I experienced was enough to make me want to have a drink or smoke a joint. But I had given all of that up and I didn't want to go back to my old habits. All I wanted was to be happy with my husband. All I wanted was for the pain and disappointment to go away. All I wanted was for the tears to stop.

The Root Of The Problem

Many years went by before I learned how to deal with my new family. But during this time, I had to also learn to deal with the reality of why I started doing drugs and drinking in the first place. After being sober for a while, the memories of my not so happy childhood, the rejection that I felt from my father, and the molestation that had occurred came flooding back into my mind, adding to the misery that I was already dealing with.

I cried a lot and I wept bitterly over my circumstances. I remember that I practically lived at the altar in my church. I took each and every altar call for anger, resentment, grief, discouragement, despair, un-forgiveness, and anything else that remotely resembled what I was going through. And by the grace of God, I was delivered from all of these things. I am finally at a point where I can handle the present hurts in my life because I have been delivered from the after effects of the past hurts in my life that I had refused to face or deal with. With God's help, I finally got to the root of the problem.

Purge The Anger From Your Past

When you have not purged your system of the anger that you still have against your father, or your mother, or anyone else that has hurt you, then any little thing that ticks you off is magnified which makes it more difficult for you to deal with life's disappointments. All of the anger that is buried deep inside of you from way back when is what is causing you so much pain today. You may find yourself crying for nothing or crying over the simplest things in life.

For Instance

Right now, you may be in a position at work where you have to deal with a difficult supervisor and you find it almost impossible to go to work everyday. You may even have a child or a stepchild who is driving you nuts, or a husband who doesn't appreciate you and is not holding true to his vows to love, honor and cherish you.

All of these things by themselves are enough to make you want to cry, but if you add them on top of unresolved anger, you have a miserable situation.

Allow God To Dry Your Tears

God sees your tears. He knows that something happened in your childhood, your young adult years or even in recent years that caused you so much grief that you did everything that you could to bury the memories. And with help from the men in your life, lots of sex, drugs, and booze, you managed to block most of what happened out of your memories.

Or maybe you never got drunk or high. Maybe you just learned how to stifle the pain. Maybe you put on your mask in public but cried tears of frustration and sadness in your private place. Maybe you stopped crying a long time ago and you're just angry. Whatever your situation, you seem to be pulling it off. You can be okay for a little while but then there are the times when a little nagging reminder triggers something on the inside of you and all hell breaks loose. Everyone that gets in your path suffers as a result of this pain that's buried deep down on the inside of your very soul.

I can relate. As I have shared with you, I've been there. And I am here to challenge you today to let it go. Face the pain and allow God to heal your heart so that you can embrace your future. God sees your pain, and He sees your tears. That's why He sent me to tell you that just like He healed the woman in the marketplace who had the issue of blood for twelve years (Mark 5:25-34), He can heal you. You see, like me and like you, this woman had been sick for a long time. Just like you and me, she had tried everything. Just like us, she had spent all of her money on medicine (or drugs, alcohol and men) that didn't do her any good. Everybody told her that her situation was hopeless. They told her that there was nothing anyone could do for her. They told her that she was stuck with this issue.

She Pressed Her Way To Jesus

Well, thank God this woman didn't believe the negative report. She had heard from the grapevine about this man named Jesus. She had heard that when people came into contact with Him, they got healed. This woman had tried everything else, so she decided to give this Jesus a try. She pressed her way to town where He was last seen and she realized that He had just passed through there. So she ran to catch up with Jesus and the crowd. Then she pushed and fought her way through the crowd and fell down at Jesus' feet grabbing the hem of His robe. The Bible says that immediately this woman was healed.

When she heard about Jesus, she came up behind him in the crowd and touched his cloak. Because she thought, "If I just touch his clothes, I will be healed." Immediately her bleeding stopped and she felt in her body that she was freed from her suffering. (Mark 5:27-29)

Tell Him About Your Troubles

Jesus turned around and asked, "Who touched me?" His disciples thought that He was crazy. *"What do you mean?"* they wanted to know. *"There are too many people here for us to tell you who touched you."* But Jesus knew who had touched Him and He stared at the woman until trembling with fear, she told Jesus all about what she had been through over the past twelve years. She told Him about her issues and about the fact that no matter what she did, nothing seemed to help. Then she told Him that she had to touch His garment because she believed that by coming into contact with Him, she would be healed. Do you know what Jesus told her? He said:

"Daughter, your faith has healed you. Go in peace and be freed from your suffering." (Mark 5:34)

This woman probably cried tears of joy when she realized that she no longer had to deal with the anguish and pain of this issue that had haunted her for so long. Jesus saw her tears. He saw her pain and He healed her. Jesus saw my tears. He saw my pain and He healed me. And just like He asked the woman to testify about her healing, He has put it upon my heart to testify about my healing. I want you to know that Jesus is seated on the throne ready and willing to heal you.

Ignore The Crowd
In order to get to Him, you've got to ignore the crowd. You've got to ignore those people who tell you that your situation is never going to get any better. You've got to ignore those people who might talk about you if you go to the altar for prayer. I'm telling you, if you will just believe that Jesus can heal your broken heart, all you have to do is run to His altar, reach out and touch the hem of His robe through prayer and tell Him all about your troubles, He will hear you

and He will heal you. He sees your tears. He sees your pain and if you let Him, He will heal you.

My Prayer For You

Lord God, I thank you for my life and I glorify your name. I thank you for seeing my tears and for healing my broken heart. I pray right now for my sister as she sits humbly before you. She is hurting God, and I have told her that you see her tears. I have told her that Jesus can heal her and that all she has to do is pray, believe, and receive the blessing of healing.

Lord God, I ask that you will give her closure on anything that hurt her in the past. I ask that you will heal her of past hurts.

Then I ask that you will give her a heart to forgive those who have hurt her. I ask that you will heal the hurt and anger of her past so that she can enjoy her present time and her future.

If it hurts too much for her to deal with some of the memories, I ask that you give her the wisdom to seek help through a counselor, a minister, or a group that is set up to help in the areas where she needs help.

But ultimately let her know that you are always with her and ready to help her in her time of need. Help her to know to call on the name of Jesus when she is overwhelmed by sadness, anger, bitterness, or resentment.

I ask that you will dry her tears as she deals with the unresolved issues in her life. I ask that you will heal her and turn her weeping into joy. In the precious name of Jesus I pray. Amen.

A WORD FROM THE LORD

Weeping may remain for a night, but rejoicing comes in the morning. – Psalm 30:5

You have cried long enough. It's morning. The sun is shining through the windows of your life. Dry your tears and take my hand. Joy awaits you.

♥ Chapter 9

The Midnight Hour

In this world you will have trouble. But take heart! I have overcome the world.

John 16:33

Who Are You?

Who are you? I mean really. Who are you when no one is looking? Are you the confident, sexy woman that every man desires? Are you the holy, pristine woman whose prayers can touch heaven? Are you the businesswoman who's reached the top? Are you the sister in the choir who can sing the paint off of the walls? Are you the usher who everyone loves? Who are you really?

Take Off The Mask

I want you to take a moment to take off your mask and then I want you to tell me, who are you in the midnight hour? You know, late at night when you're all alone and you have no one to talk to. You're lying in your bed looking at the ceiling. Or perhaps you're curled up on the couch watching one late night show after another. There are no men around to admire you, no one asking you to pray for them, no business deals to close, no audience to sing to and no congregation for you to show to their seats. Your role has been laid to the side and you have taken off the garments and the makeup that you hide behind. I want to know who are you now that there's no one around but you.

Alone In The Midnight Hour

I'm talking about the midnight hour. A time when even the married woman finds herself alone because the kids are in bed and her husband is in another room sleeping, reading the paper, working late, or watching sports on television. The midnight hour is the time when all of us are faced with facing ourselves. At the midnight hour, I have realized that I am no longer someone's mother, sister, wife, publisher, prayer partner, friend or advisor. I am now just plain old me. And at this midnight hour, when I'm all by myself, I find myself reflecting on my life. There are times when the midnight hour is unbearable.

Have you ever had a midnight hour? A time when you had to face the fact that you had feelings of bitterness and resentment in your heart? Have you ever been in the midnight hour and all of a sudden, you realized that you were still mad at someone who hurt you a long time ago, or you felt so alone that you didn't know what to do?

For those of you who are married, have you ever been in the midnight hour and felt strong feelings of dislike towards your very own husband? How about you single ladies? Have you ever been in the midnight hour and realized that your boyfriend of five years had been stringing you along and never intended to marry you? Have you ever been in a midnight hour where you were so angry or filled with grief over a lost loved one that all you could do was cry? I can raise my hand and testify that I have experienced all of these feelings at the midnight hour.

Not Just When The Clock Strikes Twelve

Now the midnight hour docs not have to be at 12:00 midnight. The midnight hour can occur at any time during your day when you look up and realize that you have some issues in your life that are evoking emotions like bitterness, sadness, anger, grief, disappointment, resentment and loneliness. Believe me, we all experience the midnight hour at some points in our lives. Some of us have a never-ending midnight hour, which causes us to live in a constant state of depression.

The Impact Of The Midnight Hour

The midnight hour can make you not want to get out of bed in the morning. The midnight hour can make you want to quit your job. The midnight hour can make you want to divorce your husband or abandon your kids.

The midnight hour can make you want to hurt someone or yourself. The midnight hour consists of the darkest periods of your life. The midnight hour can make you feel like you can't make it.

You Can't Quit

These gloomy times can make you feel like throwing up your hands and giving up. These dark times can make you want to quit. But I am here to encourage you that you can't quit. It is too soon to quit. You haven't gotten the victory yet! You see the midnight hour does not come to destroy you and keep you in darkness. The midnight hour comes to develop you and propel you towards the light.

You Can Do All Things Through Christ

You may feel like you can't go on, but I'm here to tell you that you that God will not allow you to go through anything that you can't handle. Therefore, that means that if you don't give up, you win. You can defeat depression. You can defeat bitterness. You can defeat sadness and resentment. You can defeat the spirit of divorce and discouragement in your role as a parent. You can do all things through Christ Jesus who gives you the strength to go on.

I can do everything through Him who gives me strength. (Philippians 4:13)

A Personal Testimony – My Midnight Hour

As I mentioned in the previous chapter, my midnight hour started the day after returning from my honeymoon. When our plane landed at the Newark Airport from Jamaica, I had no idea that I was facing the longest year of my life.

My husband's oldest son had made up his mind that he was not going to accept my being married to his father and his youngest son who was two years old was starting to have seizures. To make matters worse, the children's mother decided that she was going to leave the children with us and disappear into thin air for an entire year! This really rocked my newlywed world. I was in for a rocky ride and I totally was not prepared for it. For you see, Anthony had assured me that his ex-wife would never neglect or abandon her boys. Well, let me tell you. It's like she must have somehow heard our conversation and decided to do all that she could to prove him wrong.

The honeymoon was over before the marriage started. Anthony and I argued a lot about our situation and we argued even more about his oldest son's non-acceptance of me and rejection of our marriage.

I Wanted To Give Up

This went on for years. I remember many nights thinking that I wanted to give up on this child and my husband. The only thing that kept me was the fact that I had made a covenant with this man before God and God hates divorce.

So I stayed. Through the resentment, the rejection, the tears and the pain, I stayed. Through the midnight hour, I stayed. Through many midnight hours just like this one, I stayed. Over and over again, I stayed.

Then one day, years later, after many midnight hours of crying and calling out to God to heal my broken heart, He answered and it didn't hurt anymore. I had gotten the victory!

Victory Through A Changed Heart

You see, my sister, what happened after all of those years is that I stopped looking at my circumstances, and I stopped seeing myself as a victim. I stopped blaming this poor child and my husband for making me miserable, and I started looking at myself and asking God to change my heart. I asked Him to purify my emotions.

I asked God to take away the anger, the bitterness, the resentment, the sadness, the guilt, the discouragement, the anxiety over what would come next and the grief. And hallelujah! God did it! He changed my heart! He changed me and allowed me to see my circumstances through His eyes. He showed me that He gave me to my husband because my husband needed me to help him to raise his two sons.

He showed me that He gave me to my sons because they needed to be mothered and nurtured. He even showed me that their mother was not capable of being a responsible mother, and God led me to forgive her and to pray for her. He gave me a clean heart with which to worship Him. And I can tell you that I had to keep praising Him through it all. I called out to God in the midst of my despair and He gave me a peace like you wouldn't believe! God has truly changed my midnight hour into victorious joy!

It is the power of the Lord that makes you victorious!

Keys To Victory In The Midnight Hour

Acknowledge the pain, grief, or anger in your life.

Believe that God can change your situation.

Meditate on the Word of God on a regular basis.

Listen for God's voice.

Obey God's voice.

Take your eyes off of your circumstances.

Keep your eyes on Jesus.

Ask God to purify your heart.

Ask God to open your eyes so that you can see what he's trying to show you through this experience.

Forgive those who have hurt you.

Pray for strength.

Pray for those who have hurt you.

Pray for healing.

Praise God anyway. Praise Him always. Praise Him in the midnight hour and praise Him when He brings you out to see the glorious light of a new day.

After The Midnight Hour

Now when your midnight hour is over, take a good look at the lady that your dark experience has helped you to become. I guarantee you that you'll notice a change from the person that you used to be. So again I tell you that the midnight hour is not meant to harm you. Instead it is meant to mold you and to build you and to push you towards the light of a better day!

My Prayer For You

Lord God. I thank you for the midnight hours in my life. I thank you that each one of my gloomy experiences has helped me to change into the woman that you have called me to be.

I pray for my sister who is on this journey to victorious living with me. I pray for her midnight hour. Whatever it is, I submit it to you on the altar of prayer. I ask that you will give her the humility, the wisdom and the strength to make it through her midnight hour.

Lord, as she cries, let her know that her weeping will not last for long. Because you have said that when all is said and done, she will have joy in the morning.

So I thank you right now for her and I ask that you heal her of depression and cleanse her heart of all anger, bitterness, resentment, disappointment and discouragement due to shattered dreams, disillusionment, past hurts and rejection; and let her know that she is never, ever alone even when she is feeling lonely.

I ask that you give her the strength to keep her covenants and her commitments to those that she loves. Purify her heart and give her wisdom to know why you have allowed her to suffer through the midnight hour.

Lord God, I thank you for her victory. I thank you for her brighter day. In the name of Jesus Christ I pray. Amen.

A WORD FROM THE LORD

Seek me during the dark times of your life. I will turn your gloom to joy. I will give you hope, and I will give you a peace that surpasses all understanding.

♥ Chapter 10

Learning To Love Yourself

For you created me in my inmost being, you knit me together in my mother's womb. I praise you because I am fearfully and wonderfully made.
Psalm 139:13-14

Have you ever loved someone so much that you couldn't stand to be away from that person for too long? Have you ever loved someone more than you love yourself? I would like to offer that we spend our lives loving our men more than we love ourselves. Not only that, but many of us are spending years of our lives loving men that don't know how to love us.

Crazy Love

One of the reasons that we do this is primarily because we are disillusioned about what real love is and ill advised about what love is not.

Love is not desperate. Love is not being kept on the down low or being a booty call. Love is not insecure. Love is not being punched and kicked. Love is not being pushed and abandoned. Love is not cruel, harsh, abusive and unfeeling.

If you're in a relationship that is represented by any of these things, I have to put it bluntly, "That's not real love! That's crazy love!" The only reason that most of us put up with being in crazy love relationships like this is because we have not yet learned how to love ourselves.

Settling For Less

I once had very low self-esteem and I allowed myself to be in relationships with men who were no good for me. In most of these relationships, I was settling for less.

I realize now that the type of men that I was attracting was a direct reflection of what I thought of myself. I didn't think much of myself, so the men that I attracted weren't about much either. They were all in their own sense of the word, losers.

In spite of this loser status and their inability to give me the kind of love that I needed, I somehow managed to love them more than I loved myself.

Over and over again I allowed myself to waste my time trying to make something out of nothing. Therefore, I speak from experience when I say that we spend our lives loving our men more than we love ourselves.

After all, we must, or we wouldn't allow ourselves to be treated the way that we're treated in our relationships. Or better yet, if we truly loved ourselves, we wouldn't get caught up in relationships with the wrong men in the first place. We'd be able to see a loser coming.

No Losers Or Players Allowed

Finally, if we loved ourselves, we'd get to the point where the losers and the players wouldn't even approach us. And if they did, we wouldn't give them the time of day. You see, my sister, when you love yourself, you exude a certain kind of confidence.

For example, when I first started appreciating myself more, I was shocked to find that when I went to the nightclubs, the men were not coming on to me like they used to. Then I realized that it was because I was different. I looked different. I walked different. I even talked different.

One night while I was with my girlfriends, I wondered why no one had asked me to dance. I looked around me and saw that the girls who were getting the attention were the ones who wore the really short skirts and the low plunging necklines. These women were laughing loudly and acting like they had far too much to drink. They were the ones that the men were watching. That's when it hit me. Men who are on the prowl actually look for women that they can take advantage of. They are not interested in a woman who seems confident about her self. They wouldn't be able to play their little games on a woman who has her head on straight. I looked into the eyes of these men and saw something that I had never seen before – respect. That's when I realized that my life was beginning to change. I had a greater awareness of who I was and a greater love for who God had created me to be.

Love Yourself First

My experiences have taught me that you've got to love yourself before you can even begin to love someone else.

Stop being so critical of yourself and comparing yourself to other women. God created you to be just the way you are and that alone is special. You are beautiful. I know because God made you and God doesn't make junk.

You are more precious than rubies. You are a one-of-a-kind creation. There is no one on this whole earth like you. As a matter of fact, God loves you so much that He sent His own son to die for you. Now you know if God loves you that much, you've got to be pretty darn special.

Mirror, Mirror On The Wall

Stop looking in the mirror and picking apart the things that you don't like about yourself. The next time that you look in the mirror, say to yourself, "Hello beautiful. You are so radiant today. You are great. You are a phenomenal woman. I love you. I really do love you." Then go ahead and give yourself a big smile. Do this every day and see how much more you begin to appreciate yourself.

You Are All Of That

You see, we have been lied to and told so many bad things about ourselves over the years that we have actually started to believe that we are not good enough. But I'm here to set the record straight. Honey, you are all of that, a bag of chips, a diet coke and some starburst! You do have it going on and you need to believe that.

If you don't believe it, you will constantly find yourself in relationships where you are not appreciated. If you do believe it, your life will begin to change right before your very eyes.

When you love yourself, the whole world notices. When you love yourself, the abusive man and the player won't even look your way. And when you love yourself, it gives you the will and the power to get out of that bad relationship.

Your Husband Is Looking For You

When you love yourself, you are free to receive the gift of the husband that is out there looking for you. That's right, single woman, I said your husband is looking for you.

When you love yourself, you don't have to dress and act a certain way to attract attention from men. When you love yourself, you don't have to find a husband. Your husband will find you.

Speaking of husbands, when my daughter was almost four, she looked up at me and said, "Mommy, when I get big, how do I find a job, and how do I get a house, and how do I find a husband?" Her father and I looked at each other. We were shocked to hear this coming from the mouth of a baby.

Her father told her to put her mind on little girl things and that those things were grown up things, but I told her that if she did well in school and worked hard, she would get her house and her car. Then we both told her that she didn't have to worry about finding a husband because her husband would find her.

The Desires Of Your Heart

Some people would say, well it's not meant for everyone to be married. I agree, but if it's a desire of your heart to be married, then it's meant for you to be married. My Bible tells me that if we delight ourselves in the Lord, He will give us the desires of our heart *(Psalm 37:4)*. I interpret this scripture like this: When we seek God with our whole heart, He will deposit what His will is for our lives into our heart. That leads me to believe that it is God who gives us the desire to get married in the first place, and after all, marriage is a covenant that is ordained by God. Therefore, if a daughter of God wants to be married, God will send her husband to find her. Hallelujah! The Bible says that he who finds a wife finds a good thing and obtains favor from the Lord *(Proverbs 18:22)*. Shift your focus from finding a husband to being the good thing that God created you to be.

Then you will have the favor of the Lord resting on you and when your husband does find you, he in turn will be a blessed man.

You've Got To Be Ready

It is important that you are prepared for the appointed time when your husband comes a courting. Here are some things that are absolutely necessary for you to already have in place before you consider getting married.

1) You must be grateful for the person that God has created you to be.

2) You must make sure that you have been healed of the wounds from the past.

3) You must have forgiven all who have hurt you in the past.

4) You must have a pure heart that's open to give love and receive the love of a husband, and

5) You must have eyes of discernment that will help you to recognize that this is the man that God has sent for you.

Get Rid Of Your Shopping List

Don't be crazy enough to give God your shopping list for a husband. You know the kind of list that I'm talking about. *"Well, God, I want my husband to be tall, dark and handsome. And I want him to have a white-collar job. And ooh God, can you make him rich? I mean, I don't want no man that drives a station wagon. Let him drive a Lexus, God. And I want him to be built just like Arnold Schwarzenagger. And no kids God. Please don't let him have kids."*

And then when the average looking brother who runs a mechanic shop asks you out, you turn up your nose and turn him down. When the brother who drives an old, beat up car asks you to lunch, you make an excuse not to go. And when the short, balding brother from the choir asks you to dinner, you tell him that you have a man. Yet, you keep asking God to send you a husband. But God has already sent you three men and one of them could have been your husband. But since none of them matched the criteria from your list, you didn't even consider going out with them.

Don't Try To Put God In A Box!

It is a foolish woman that passes over blessings from God repeatedly. Holding on to your selfish preferences leaves little room for God to move.

111

Ask God For Wisdom

Sister, you must stop the nonsense. Stop trying to put limits on God. Stop trying to choose your own husband. If God is really in control, let God choose the man that you're to marry. Pray and ask Him to give you the wisdom to know who to go to lunch with or who to have a cup of coffee with. I'll give you a hint. If the man is saved, single, and serving the Lord, it may be a good idea to accept his offer to have lunch or a cup of coffee. Girl, you'd better act like you know!

Finally, when God's plan is revealed and your husband has found you, you must be able to love him. The only way that you're going to be able to love anyone is by first being able receive God's love in your life and secondly by being able to love yourself.

My Prayer For You

Lord God, I thank you for my sister and the fact that she is learning to love herself. I pray that she will be able to look into the mirror and see herself the way that you see her. God, reveal her true beauty to her, both inside and out. I ask that you will show her that when the issues of her heart have been healed, then she will be able to radiate the true beauty of a whole, healed, spirit filled person, and that this glow will radiate and attract the type of people that you have ordained to be in her life.

Then, I ask you to help her to heal the heart issues of fear, low self-esteem, bitterness, any hint of un-forgiveness, shame, and guilt. Show my sister that she does not need a husband to make her whole, but that she indeed needs to be whole in order to be a wife.

Reveal to her that she is a prize and that she is valuable in your sight. Show her that she is worth far more than the most precious of jewels with or without a man in her life. I pray that you will help my sister to walk with boldness into the destiny that you prepared for her even before she was born. Renew her sense of self through your Word and let her begin to reflect this in everything that she does and in every relationship in her life.

I thank you for the victory in my sister's life as she walks away from those relationships that do not glorify you and as she turns her back on the players and losers that have tried to block her true blessings that are coming from you. I thank you and I praise you for the work that you are doing in my sister's life. In the name of your son, Jesus, I pray. Amen.

A WORD FROM THE LORD

I created you in my image. You are awesome to behold. You are not a finished work. I am still working on you. When you are fully mature in the Kingdom, you will look like me. Love yourself for who you are today. Love yourself because I took great care in creating you. Know that you are special; a radiant jewel for my glory.

♥ Chapter 11

Sick And Tired Of Being Sick And Tired

Come to me all who are weary and burdened, and I will give you rest. - Matthew 11:28

Have you gotten to the point in your life yet where you're sick and tired of being sick and tired? I have. It is when we get to this point that we begin to look around for ways to change our lives.

A Personal Testimony

As I mentioned earlier in this book, there was a time in my life when I was on welfare. It came to the point where I was twenty-one years old and had been on welfare for almost five years.

My baby girl had just turned five and I remember not getting my monthly welfare check in the mail. So I dropped my daughter off at my mother's and headed over to the local welfare office. When I got off of the bus and walked over to the building, I saw a whole bunch of guys standing on the outside of the building. They were smoking cigarettes and talking amongst each other while they waited for the women inside. When I walked by them, I could tell that they were staring at me, and a couple of them even whistled. I ignored them and kept going into the building. My focus was on finding out why I didn't get my usual monthly check in the mail. I gave my name to the receptionist and she told me to sit down and wait until I was called.

I Felt Like I Didn't Belong

As I sat in the smoke-filled room, I felt like I didn't belong there. I looked around at the women in the crowded room. Most of them looked like they had just crawled out of the bed. Their heads were covered with dingy bandanas and they smoked one cigarette after another as they watched the talk show on the television set. Some of them had children with them. Most of these kids looked older than five or six, and I remember wondering why they were not in school. The kids ran around the office making noise and their mothers ignored them.

Where's My Money?

After I had been in the welfare office for over an hour, one of the women started screaming at her caseworker. "Where's my money? Where's my blank blank money?" she yelled at the top of her lungs. The caseworker tried to explain why she didn't get the check and told her that it would be mailed. The woman just started screaming louder, "No. You're going to give me my blank blank money! I'm not leaving here until you give me my check!"

I was so embarrassed by this woman cursing out the caseworker. I remember thinking she had not earned one dime of that money, yet she had the nerve to curse someone out because she didn't get a check in the mail. It was at that moment that I knew for sure that I didn't belong there anymore. I made a vow to myself that I would not be coming back to the welfare office.

Time To Find A Job

Now don't get me wrong. Everyone in the welfare office was not unkempt or rowdy. There were women there who were immaculate in their dress. But it was the rowdy ones that helped me to make my decision to get out of the welfare system. Besides, the welfare system helped me when I was a sixteen-year-old mother, but it had come to a point, five years later, when it was time for me to get off of my young able butt and find a J.O.B.

I've Never Looked Back

When I was called into the back, I told the caseworker that I wanted to go to work and she helped me to get into a program that did job assessment. I tested so well, that the people at the Job Training and Assessment Program gave me a job with on-the-job training in computers. That was where I got my start in administrative work and I have never looked back. I kept looking forward and upward at bigger and better opportunities until I finally landed a job at Merrill Lynch. At this company, I was able to earn enough money to move my child and myself into a nice neighborhood without roaches and mice.

Limited Choices

I told you this to make a point. The point is that I actually stayed on welfare for five years before realizing that there had to be a better way. Although the money that I was getting only allowed me to live in low-income housing where the living conditions were not that great, it took me that long to get motivated enough to get my butt moving. I was never happy living under such substandard conditions, but I felt too limited in my choices to make a change. I mean, what could I do? I was a high school dropout with no work history other than some factory work here and there.

Tired Enough To Make A Change

This experience showed me that when you get sick and tired enough of living a substandard life, you will make a change. It's not enough to be tired of being on welfare, tired of being poor, tired of being neglected, tired of being used, tired of being abused, tired of being looked over for a promotion, tired of going to a job that you hate everyday, tired of being angry, tired of being drunk, or tired of being on drugs, but you have to be sick and tired of being sick and tired. When you get to that point, you will make a change.

You Have To Believe That You Deserve Better

You have to believe that you were not created to live a substandard life. You don't have to settle for less. God has given you the gift of an abundant life.

This is a life filled with everything that you need to make it in this world with some luxuries thrown in. You are not a pauper. You are a child of God and that makes you royalty. God, who is your heavenly Father, owns the whole world and everything in it and He wants you to have the abundant life. All you have to do is make up your mind that you are not going to settle for less anymore.

Take A Leap Of Faith

Step out on faith and begin to live the life that you have only dreamed about. If God has given you an idea for starting a company or if you have always dreamed of writing a book, now is the time to do it. God has given you everything that you need to make it in this world. He has deposited gifts on the inside of each and every one of us that can be utilized to get wealth. The Bible says that God has given us the ability to get wealth *(Deut. 8:18)*.

Begin To Make Changes Today

If you have been overlooked time and time again for a promotion, it may be time to begin sending your resume to other companies. If you are in a relationship with someone who treats you badly, it is time to have a serious talk with that person and let him know that he has to start doing right by you. Chances are that you will have to kick him to the curb. Here's a hint. If you have been with a man for over two years and he still won't commit or has no interest in marriage, then it's time for you to move on. My Pastor, Bishop Hilliard always says that it does not take a man more than a year to figure out if you're the one. I wholeheartedly agree!

Stop Playing House

Here's another hint. If you are doing his cooking, cleaning, washing and ironing his clothes and keeping his sexual appetite satisfied, he has no reason to commit to you or marry you. You are already giving him everything he would get in a marriage, and he doesn't even have to give you the satisfaction of allowing you to be his wife.

There's an old saying that a man won't buy the cow if he can get the milk for free. Most of us heard this growing up but we had no idea what it meant. Simply put, if the man is getting sex from you anytime he wants to – morning, noon, and night – he's not likely to marry you. Why should he make that kind of investment when he can get the goodies for free?

A lot of us are even having babies for men that are married or men who are living with another woman. What's up with that? When did we get so desperate that we would settle for being second best?

Been There, Done That

I must tell you that I've been there, done that, got the t-shirt. I've settled for lies and being the other woman. I've sat home by the phone on weekends and hit the highway three or four times during the week to answer a booty call. I've done it and I'm not proud of it. But I thank God that one day I got sick and tired of being kept on the Down Low, sick and tired of being on welfare, sick and tired of being a booty call, sick and tired of being with men who didn't deserve the time of day from me, sick and tired of being high, sick and tired of being drunk, sick and tired of being insignificant. But most of all I'm glad that I became sick and tired of being sick and tired and made the choice to make some changes in my life.

Are You Sick And Tired Yet?

You may be able to relate to all of this and you may even be at the point where you are sick and tired of being sick and tired.

If you are, I'm here to tell you that there is a way out. You have been through all that you've been through to bring you to this point. You see, Jesus tells us to come to Him. All who are weary and heavy burdened and He will give us rest *(Matthew 11:28)*.

God Will Help You

If you bring your burdens to the Lord and cast your cares on him, He will help you to make the changes in your life that you need to make. He will give you peace and He will give you joy. He will give you the Holy Spirit, and the Holy Spirit will give you the power to go from being sick and tired to being victorious. He will give you a new life, a new mind, and a new heart.

I'm not talking religious gibberish. I'm speaking Biblical truth and I speak from experience. You see I was once at the point of being tired of the way that I was living my life, I was tired of having no hope and my future didn't look too bright.

Then one night on a New Year's Eve, I heard a song that went something like this, "Come to Jesus. He'll take good care of you. Come to Jesus. He'll make your life brand new." And then Bishop Hilliard at the Cathedral did an alter call and I found myself at the alter accepting this promise for my life. Now you have to realize that it was customary for me to be falling off of a barstool and kissing drunk friends and strangers when the clock struck twelve in previous years on New Year's Eve.

A Brand New Life

Now ten years later, I can tell you that my life is brand new. I stopped hanging out in bars from that night on. My anger, resentment and bitterness were replaced by joy and peace. I was able to forgive all of the people that had hurt me. I quit my job in Corporate America and started my own company and I wrote and published my first novel. I have a wonderful husband and four great kids. We have a home in a nice neighborhood. My relationship with my oldest daughter was restored beyond what I can imagine. My relationship with my mother and sisters is better than it's ever been. I have not had any drugs in over ten years and I haven't had a drink in over eight years. I have a greater awareness of who I am and I am happy. I am so happy sometimes that I wonder if I'm dreaming.

Now don't get me wrong. I didn't just accept Jesus into my heart and my life was automatically perfect. As a matter of fact, my life is not perfect now nor will it ever be. I still have some hard times. But because I seek to hear from God through prayer and studying His Word daily, my life is much better than it was before I turned it all over to God.

God Can Do It For You Too

God is no respecter of persons. You too can begin to make the changes for a better life. If you're sick and tired of being sick and tired, I'm here to serve notice that you don't have to live like that anymore. There is a better way and the way is Jesus. If you just believe and allow Jesus to direct your paths, He will begin to guide you to make the necessary changes. As you draw nearer to Jesus, He will give you a bigger desire to change and He will empower you to change.

I'm Saved But My Life Is Still A Mess

You may already be saved and you may be saying, "Come on sister Rebecca. I've been saved for a long time and my life is still a mess. Then I would like to submit to you that perhaps you are not totally sold out for Jesus. Could it be a possibility that you have not fully submitted your life to Jesus your Savior and made Him Jesus your Lord, or is it that maybe you need to spend more time studying the

Word of God and learning about His plans for your life? Maybe you can spend more time in prayer or praise and worship so that you can hear the voice of God. Ask God to show you the areas in your relationship with Him that need to be improved upon. Then ask Him to give you a heart to obey His voice and the courage to step out on faith and do what He tells you to do, especially if He tells you to quit smoking or drinking, spend less money, drop a trifling man, get a new job, start a business or buy a new house.

This Super Religious Stuff Is Not For Me

You may be totally against 'religion' and you may be saying, "Come on Rebecca. I don't believe that stuff." To you my sister, I would like to respond that I totally understand where you're coming from. I once felt the same way. But, if you've tried everything else and none of that stuff has worked, I suggest that you go ahead and give Jesus a try.

Someone once said that insanity is doing things the way you've always done things and expecting the outcome to be different. If nothing else has worked and you still refuse to believe that perhaps God can change your life for the better, then I would have to submit that you are not sick and tired of being sick and tired. You haven't gotten to that point yet.

Commit Your Whole Life To God

In any case, if you really want to make a change I would advise both the sister who is saved and the sister who is skeptical about all of this God stuff to commit your whole life to God.

Go ahead. Repent of your sins and ask Jesus to come into your life and take over. Tell Him that you are going to submit and allow Him to change everything in you that needs to be changed. Read the Gospel of John so that you can get to know more about Jesus' ministry. Pray to God every day and every night. Pray to Him when you feel lost or discouraged. Go to weekly church worship services. Praise the Lord with all of your mind and all of your heart. Give your tithes and offering. Follow the prompting of the Holy Spirit and watch the Lord turn your whole world around.

God will change your love life, your family life, your financial picture, your health, your heart and your mindset. If you tap into the power of God, you will begin to make changes for the better in your life. You will be empowered by the Holy Spirit to change.

I'm a living testimony. Jesus is not a fairy tale. Jesus is real and He will transform you into the wonderful, joy-filled, powerful, successful, purpose-filled woman that you were born to be.

My Prayer For You

Lord God, I humbly come before you praising your holy name. I thank you for coming into my life at a time when I was sick and tired of being sick and tired. I thank you for getting me off of welfare, and giving me the ability to create wealth in my life. I thank you for keeping me through the storms of life and for showing me my true value.

I pray right now for my sister. For she is now at the point where she is sick and tired of being on welfare, or she is sick and tired of working at a job where she is not appreciated, she is sick and tired of all of the failed relationships.

She is sick and tired of the men that she's been dealing with. She is sick and tired of being used and abused. Show her that she is better than that. Show her that she deserves to be treated better than that. Show my sister that she can achieve all of the things that she ever dreamed of if she will just have faith in you.

Lord God, I pray right now that my sister will turn her whole heart and her whole life over to you. I pray that she will begin to see the path that she should take. I pray that she will be motivated to get out of the rut that she's in.

I pray that she will seek your face daily and that you will give her wisdom and favor in her life. I thank you for my sister right now, Lord. And I ask you to do a new thing in her life. Make her life brand new as she comes to you on bended knees. Bring her to a point where she is no longer sick and tired but living the victorious life that you intended for her to live. In the name of Jesus I pray. Amen.

A WORD FROM THE LORD

My daughter. You are blessed and highly favored. I will do a new thing in your life. Come unto me and partake of all that I have in store for you.

♥ Chapter 12

You Don't Have To Live Like That

You were taught, with regard to your former way of life, to put off your old self, which is being corrupted by its deceitful desires; to be made new in the attitude of your minds; and to put on the new self, created to be like God in true righteousness and holiness.

Ephesians 4:22-24

You don't have to live like that. You don't have to live in abusive relationships. You don't have to live your life addicted to drugs. You don't have to live your life going from bed to bed and man to man. You don't have to live your life depending on alcohol or sex to make you feel better. You don't have to live sick and tired of being sick and tired.

You don't have to live like that!

You can have a better life. You don't have to spend your life looking for stuff and people to quench a thirst or a hunger that you have deep down on the inside of your soul. You don't have to live hungry for love and thirsty for attention.

The Woman At The Well

The Bible tells us about a woman that Jesus met at the well *(John 4:1-26)*. This woman had been married five times and she was living with a man who was not her husband. She had come to the well to get some water and there she met Jesus.

Jesus spoke to her and asked her to give Him something to drink. She was amazed that He was asking her for water. Since she was considered to be a low life. Jesus told her that if she knew who He was, she would ask Him to give her some water. He told her that once she tasted of the water that He had, she would never thirst again. He told her to go and get her husband and she told Him that she wasn't married.

Jesus replied that He knew she was telling the truth and He even told her about the man that she was living with. Immediately, this woman wanted the water that Jesus had told her about.

She received it and went on telling everyone what had happened at the well. She told them all about this Jesus that knew everything that she had ever done. You see, Jesus saw the way that this woman was living and He wasn't going to let her continue to try to quench her thirst with sex and men, so He offered her a better way. He offered her living water and she accepted it.

Jesus Sees You Too

Jesus also sees the way that you are living, and He wants to offer you the same living water that He offered to this woman at the well. There's no use in pretending with Jesus because He already knows all about you. He knows about your pain, your fears, your disappointments, and your heartaches. He knows about your mistakes and your desire for a better way. He knows. Believe me, He knows.

He personally met this woman at the well way back then. But in this day and time, He sends people to meet you where you least expect it so that they can tell you about His goodness and His mercy. He sent a man to meet me in a bar. He sent me to meet you in this book. The Bible says that once you receive Jesus into your heart, streams of living water will flow from your belly *(John 7:38)*. That living water represents abundant, victorious life. That living water represents love, peace and joy in the Holy

Spirit that can only be found in the Kingdom of God. Have you received this living water? Have you received the salvation of the Lord and the forgiveness of your sins? If not, you can do so today. You don't have to wait to go to church. Right here and right now you can say this prayer:

Lord God, forgive me of my sins. Come into my heart. I believe that Jesus died so that I can live. Heal my broken heart. Make me brand new. Give me your living water. In the name of Jesus I pray. Amen.

Congratulations! You have now officially received the forgiveness of God for your sins and the gift of the Holy Spirit that comes to live on the inside of every believer. If you allow Him to, God will make your life brand new.

Therefore, if anyone is in Christ, he or she is a new creation, the old has gone, the new has come! (2 Corinthians 5:17)

You don't have to live in poverty and doubt and fear. You don't have to live like that. As a believer of the Lord Jesus Christ, you are entitled to a better life. You are entitled to victorious living. Walk into your destiny now and don't look back.

A Closer Walk With God

If you are already a believer but find yourself living with fornication, abuse, addictions, neglect, unwillingness to forgive, poverty, doubt and fear, you can change all of that by taking a closer walk with God. It's time to stop straddling the fence. You must turn your back on all of the things that are keeping you hostage and hindering you from having an abundant life *(Hebrews 12:1)*. You know that God told you to stop living with your boyfriend when you first got saved. Now it's five years later and you're still living with him, still waiting for him to marry you.

As the angel of the Lord told Lot and his wife, get out and don't look back *(Genesis 19:17)*. Unfortunately, Lot's wife looked back and was turned into a pillar of salt. Now you may not be turned into a pillar of salt if you look back or if you don't get out, but you will definitely miss out on the blessings that the Lord has for you if you stay.

Obedience Equals Blessings

The key to abundant, victorious living is total obedience to the voice of God. When God speaks, it's always for your own good. He's not trying to take anything from you. He's trying to get His blessings to you. So today, just like the new believer, you can start afresh by cleaning the old stuff of the world out of your life and embracing the blessings that God's been trying to give you.

You don't have to live like that. Today is a new day. Today is the first day of the rest of your life. Turn away from the lifestyle that you know does not please God. If the truth were to be told, your lifestyle doesn't even please you. Yes, it may be hard to turn your back on the way that you've lived all of your life. You may even be afraid of losing yourself. But I would like to offer to you that if you keep doing things the way you've been doing them, you're going to keep getting the same results that you've been getting. I would like to offer to you that you have tried everything else, you might as well try it God's way! I understand your position. I've been there. But one day, I decided to surrender my will to the will of God. And I must tell you that I love what God has done in my life since I turned it all over to Him. Now that I've received His blessings, I'll never go back to living the way that I was before I met Jesus.

Have a Drink Of Living Water

Jesus is offering you a drink of water that will change your whole life – for the better. Why not take a sip and see how good it tastes? You won't regret it. Let this continuous stream of water wash you from the inside out. You'll find that you no longer have a desire for the things that you depended on to make you happy before.

This one little sip of water will taste so good that you'll want to drink more and more until you're filled with a joy like you've never experienced before.

Walk With The Lord

Keep walking with the Lord by praying, reading His Word in the Bible and acting on His Word. You'll be a new person if you only allow yourself to be transformed by the renewing of your mind. You must allow your way of thinking to be replaced by God's way of thinking *(Romans 12:2)*.

You don't have to live a life of lack, sadness, and despair. You don't have to live like that. But don't just take my word for it. Try Jesus, I mean really try Him, and see for yourself.

My Prayer For You

Lord God, I thank you for saving my life. I thank you that you saw the way that I was living and decided to send someone to offer me a drink of your living water.

And I pray for my sister right now. I pray that she will receive this same living water that will give her a fresh, new life. I thank you for the prayer that she has prayed and I ask that you seal it in her life. I pray that she has already tasted of the living water through this prayer and that she will take the time to drink deeply of it.

I pray that you will open her eyes to show her that she doesn't have to live in poverty, shame, fear, guilt or sin of any kind. I pray that she will receive your forgiveness and move on to the abundant life that you have prepared for her. Lord God, I pray that she will turn from the lifestyle that is not pleasing to you, the lifestyle that is destroying her soul and that she will turn to the lifestyle of abundance, love, and joy that can be found in your Holy Spirit.

Fill her with the Holy Spirit so that your joy and power can be found overflowing in her life. I thank you that you have made a way out of no way and that my sister is not stuck in this trap that has been her life. I thank you that you have sent your son to walk with and speak to those who are considered to be low lives. I thank you that your son, Jesus, gives those same people new lives.

I glorify your Holy name and I thank you for the work that you've done in my life and the work that's yet to be done. I also thank you for the work that you will do in my sister's life. I glorify your name and I give you praise. Amen.

A WORD FROM THE LORD

I died so that you could have life and have it in abundance. Put away the old things that you have used in the past to make you feel better. Leave the old harmful behavior behind, and walk in the newness of life that I have already provided for you.

♥ Chapter 13

Standing When You Feel Like Falling

Therefore put on the full armor of God, so that when the day of evil comes, you may be able to stand your ground and after you have done everything, to stand.

Ephesians 6:13

What do you do when your whole life seems to be falling apart around you? Your husband or your boyfriend breaks up with you when you thought that everything was fine. You got laid off from your job. You don't have enough money to pay your bills. Your teen-age son was just picked up with drugs in his possession. You just found out that your fifteen-year-old daughter is pregnant and has dropped out of high school. Your sister can't stand you. Your brother is in Iraq fighting in a war where people are being killed every day. Your doctor has given you a bad report and to top it all off, you have just buried a loved one.

You may be standing right now at a point where you don't think that you can make it. The devil is a liar! You can make it! Stay with me, I want to share another testimony with you.

A Personal Testimony

I have had many seasons in my life that are very similar to the ones that I talked about in the previous section. If I can be totally transparent with you, I must tell you that there have been times in my life, even in my Christian life, when I felt like just throwing up my hands in frustration and quitting.

During one of these times, I had just found out that my daughter had been cutting school and was pregnant with her third baby. My rent on my apartment was past due, my sister hated my guts, and I still had a lot of emotional issues that I was dealing with. I remember standing in the hallway of my small apartment wondering what I was going to do. I had just started going to church and I actually remember saying to one of my friends that my life was better before I got saved then it was now that I was saved. I told him that it would have been better if I had never gotten involved in all of this Jesus stuff. He mentioned something about a spiritual attack and the enemy. But in my young spiritual mind, I couldn't understand how I was supposed to be saved and still be going through more hell than I ever had in my life. At least that's the way it seemed. It seemed like all of a sudden, I was under this immense attack from some unseen forces. I mean, really, can you relate to this at all?

Were Things Better Before?

I am confident that someone out there can definitely relate to feeling like it would have been easier to stay on the barstool, drinking until everything was numb. Someone is alone tonight, again. And you are feeling like it would have been better for you if you had stayed in that adulterous relationship. At least you had him some of the time. And after all, isn't half a man better than none at all?

Someone is feeling like you should have stayed in that relationship where you knew that he was just using you to satisfy his sexual needs. After all, it wasn't *all* bad and at least you got to feel the comfort of a man's arms around you sometimes. Some of you are feeling like you should have kept cheating on your taxes. You didn't have to pay so much when you lied a little bit and sometimes you even got a refund.

Someone else is feeling like maybe it would have been better to keep doing drugs. At least when you were high you didn't have to deal with the frustration of trying to cope with this thing called life.

Thinking About Turning Back

Have you ever been there? I have and I must admit, just like the people of Israel in the Bible, I thought that it might have been better had I stayed in Egypt. Even though the people were slaves in Egypt. And even though they were mistreated and misused and abused, once they crossed the Red Sea, they looked back and grumbled that maybe they just should have stayed where they were *(Exodus 16)*. At least life was predictable then. Although the Egyptians treated them badly, at least they got to eat some of their choice foods. And they didn't have the responsibility of worrying about taking care of themselves or dealing with the issues of life that were threatening to overwhelm them. Oh yeah, I felt just like the Israelites, and I even grumbled that maybe, just maybe, I should have stayed. I'm telling you. I was having a hard time coping and I wanted to QUIT.

The Keeping Power Of The Holy Spirit

But God, in His infinite wisdom, by the divine intervention of His Holy Spirit kept prompting me to go on. The Word of the Lord kept encouraging me not to grow weary in doing good. For in due season, if I didn't give up I was going to reap my reward for staying faithful *(Galatians 6:9)*. God reminded me in His Word that He was with me and that I was never alone.

Because God Has said, "Never Will I leave you; Never Will I Forsake you." – (Hebrews 13:5)

He assured me that I didn't have to worry about how my everyday, basic needs would be met. He showed me the lilies of the fields and told me that He would provide for me better than He had the lilies of the field and that He cared much more about me than He cared about the birds of the air.

Look at the birds of the air; they do not sow or reap or store away in barns, and yet your heavenly Father feeds them. Are you not much more valuable than they? And why do you worry about clothes? See how the lilies of the field grow. They do not labor or spin. Yet I tell

145

you that not even Solomon in all of his splendor was dressed like one of these. If that is how God clothes the grass of the field, will he not much more clothe you? So do not worry saying what shall we drink or what shall we wear? (Matthew 6:26,28-31)

He told me not to worry about my problems, but that I should bring all of my concerns to Him in prayer.

Do not be anxious about anything, but in everything, by prayer and petition, with thanksgiving, present your request to God. And the peace of God, which transcends all understanding, will guard your hearts and your minds in Christ Jesus. (Philippians 4:6)

He told me not to worry about tomorrow because tomorrow has enough worries of it's own

Therefore, do not worry about tomorrow, for tomorrow will worry about itself. Each day has enough trouble of its own. (Matthew 6:34)

As for my daughter God showed me that she belonged to Him too. Because my Bible tells me that the earth is the Lord's and the fullness thereof, and everybody on earth belongs to Him too.

The earth is the Lord's and everything in it, the world, and all who live in it. (Psalm 24:1)

So I was comforted in knowing that He was going to take care of her and those babies too.

Apply The Promises Of God

Oh yes, I'm talking about standing when you feel like falling. If you're at a point in your walk with God where you're getting a little discouraged, apply all of these promises to your own life. God has given us His Word to be a lamp unto our feet. His Word is to guide us and to remind us of His great love for us. God is not a man that He should lie. In other words, He is not like all of the other men in your life who have lied to you and let you down. God will never let you down. He is right there in the middle of your dilemma with you. He knows that you are thinking about giving up and going back to your old friends and your old habits. It's only natural that you would be tempted to go back. Just like the people of Israel, we will always be more comfortable with the familiar as opposed to the unfamiliar. We know what we left behind and we only have promises of what's ahead of us.

The Israelites had the promise of freedom from their bondage. They had the promise of a land flowing with milk and honey to look forward to, but the journey was becoming too much for them. They were tired of being in the dry place, and they wanted to hurry up and have the life that God had promised them. Just like the people of Israel, we get tired of the dry places. We don't want to take a journey and walk with God until we get to where he's leading us. We want to skip all of the hardships and tests and get right to the good stuff. Right? I know I'm right because I was there. But I am so happy that I didn't go back. I am happy that I kept going to the chapel and getting prayed for because I wasn't mature enough to pray for myself.

Encouragement For Your Dry Place

I want to encourage you, my sister. I know that you're in a dry place right now. I know that it's also a hard place and you can't see how you're going to get through it. But the great thing about God's grace and His mercy is that we don't have to know how God is going to bring us through it. All we have to do is trust God and believe that He will do it! Trust God.

Although you feel like falling or you feel like you might go under, stand firm on the promises in His Word and He will bring you through victorious. You see there is no weapon that can come against you that will prosper *(Isaiah 54:17)*.

You Will Not Be Defeated

Although you are pressed down on every side, you will not be defeated, unless you allow yourself to be. Although your mother and father let you down, that's okay because God will never leave you or forsake you. Your husband may have walked out on you, but you're going to be okay because God's Word says that He will not allow you to go through any more than you can handle. Girl, God's got your back.

No temptation has seized you except what is common to man. And God is faithful; he will not let you be tempted beyond what you can bear. But when you are tempted, he will also provide a way out so that you can stand up under it.
(I Corinthians 10:13)

Stand On His Promises

"Well, sister Rebecca," you may say. "That's all well and fine. But how do I stand on God's Word when I feel like falling?" In response I say to you, my sister, that you can do all things because it is Christ Jesus who strengthens you. I say that if you will humble yourself and pray, the Lord will hear you and He will heal your situation and your home and your body. I say that if you just believe, God will give you the grace to make it through this time in your life. I say, it may not seem possible for you, but with God all things are possible. I'm saying lift up your eyes to the hills. In other words take your eyes off of your situation and lift your eyes towards heaven. Pray and praise the Lord for what He's going to do. He has already assured you that the fervent prayers of the righteous reach His ears and make a difference *(James 5:16)*. Pray, praise, believe God and worship Him with your whole heart and your whole life. Know His Word and stand on His promises. I guarantee you that the Lord will bring you through!

Just stand! God will bring you through!

My Prayer For You

Lord God, I thank you for bringing me through the dry places of my walk. I thank you that you didn't allow me to turn back to the things that I had left behind.

I pray for my sister reading this right now. I thank you for bringing her out of darkness. I thank you for saving her and turning her life around. Because I know that it's not always easy to walk this Christian walk, I ask that you will keep her mind focused on your Word. I ask that you will give her a heart to be like a tree planted by the streams of your living water so that everything she does will prosper.

I ask that you help her during the early stages of her walk, that you will carry her through the hard times, that you will inspire her to have an intimate relationship with you, that you will give a heart to obey your Word, that you will keep her from the temptation of going back to the world and that you will help her to grow up to be a mature woman of God.

I thank you that you can make a way out of what seems like no way and I praise you because it is only you who can keep us standing when we feel like falling. I ask you to give my sister strength and to keep her on the path that your Word has ordered for her.

I thank you for answered prayers and the promises of your Word. My sister and I both praise you. We worship and adore you, and we are glad to be called your children. In the name of Jesus I pray. Amen.

A WORD FROM THE LORD

When you feel like falling, lean on me. I will hold you up with my right hand. Have faith in me. Keep your eyes on me. Don't focus on your problems or the people in your life who are causing you to worry. Live your life for me and I will take care of you.

♥ Chapter 14

The Road To Victory

Trust in the Lord with all your heart and lean not on your own understanding; in all your ways acknowledge him, and he will make your paths straight. – Proverbs 3:5-6

Well here we are standing here together, on the road to victory. We have come a mighty long way and we are almost at the point of victorious living. I would like to take the time here to share some final victory points with you.

Victory Point #1: In order to have victory in life you must know who you are. You are not a hoochie mama, a booty call, a whore, a slut, a chicken, a video ho, or any other profane thing that you may have been called. You are a woman of God. You are a child of God. You are a queen. You are more precious than any jewel. You are fearfully and wonderfully made in the image of God. You are one of a kind. You are a virtuous woman. You are beautiful. You are full of wisdom. You are awesome.

Victory Point #2: Your life is filled with both promise and possibilities. There is no dream that you cannot achieve. In order to have victory in life you must avoid the dream killers. The dream killers are doubt, insecurity, fear, negative people and negative thinking. Trust in God and He will give you the desires of your heart.

Victory Point #3: In order to have victory in life, you must love and value the God who created you. And you must love and value yourself as a child of God. You must refuse to allow anyone to mistreat you or abuse you. You must recognize that your body is a temple of God and you must not dishonor that temple with sex outside of marriage, drugs, alcohol, cigarette smoking, or excessive junk food.

Victory Point #4: In order to have victory in life, you must forgive those who have hurt you. Most importantly you must forgive yourself for the things that you have done that were wrong in the past. With God, you are now a new creation and old things have passed away. God has forgiven you. In order to have victory in life, you must accept that forgiveness and move on with your life. Don't get caught in the traps of shame and guilt and don't look back. Look forward and allow the Word of God to guide your footsteps.

Victory Point #5: In order to have victory in life, you must renew your mind by daily reading the Word of God in the Bible. You must allow this Word to penetrate your mind and your heart, and you must ask God to change you from the inside out.

Victory Point #6: In order to have victory in life, you must praise the Lord at all times, through the good times and the bad.

Victory Point #7: In order to have victory in life, you have to pray continually, asking God to help you with everything in your life.

Victory Point #8: In order to have victory in life, you must use your resources (time, talent, and money) in and out of the house of God to help others to have victory in life through Jesus.

Victory Point #9: In order to have victory in life, you must be obedient to the Lord, worshipping Him not only in the song and praise but also in your everyday living. Your whole life should be lived as an expression of worship, which is only done by doing those things that you know are pleasing to God.

Victory Point #10: In order to have victory in life, you must never, ever give up. You have to refuse to quit. You have to be determined that you are going to have victory in life. Even when things look bad, remember that you're with Jesus.

Traveling Down The Road With Jesus

I'm reminded of Jairus from the Bible *(Mark 5:22-43)*. His daughter was dying and he went and found Jesus and asked Him to come to his house to heal his daughter. As they were walking down the road to his house, some people came and told Jairus that he might as well give up on having Jesus come because the girl was dead.

I can imagine the look of shock and anguish on Jarius' face as he looked first at his friends and then at Jesus. Ignoring Jairus' friends, Jesus told him, "Don't be afraid. Just believe." I can see Jairus as he pondered what he should do. Was he going to believe the negative report or was he going to go on with Jesus? The story goes on to tell us that Jairus kept on walking with Jesus and when they got to his house Jesus kicked out all of those who had a negative mindset and healed the little girl. I told you this story to tell you that if Jairus had believed the report of his friends, he would have given up on Jesus. His daughter probably would have died and he would not have gotten the victory in his life.

What Are You Going To Do?

So I ask you. What are you going to do? Are you going to cast aside fear, doubt, disbelief, negative thinking and negative reports from unbelievers and keep walking with Jesus or are you going to continue believing what other people tell you? Are you going to give in to your own insecurities and quit or are you going to keep pressing forward believing that with Jesus, you can be the winner that you were born to be?" The choice is yours. There is an old saying that you can lead a horse to water, but you can't make him drink. By the same token, you can tell a person how to have victory, but you can't make them take action on your advice. I have done my part and I've done it with love for you in my heart. I care about what happens to you. I want you to have victory in life. I really do.

Now what do you want? We're already on the road to victory. Are you going to continue with Jesus or are you going to turn back and take what seems to be the easy way out? The Bible says that there is a way that seems right to a person, but the end of that path is death *(Proverbs 14:12)*. Take a good look down the road that you've been traveling. Where does it lead? Is it leading to death? Now take a good look down the road of victory that God has laid out for you. Where do you think it's going to take you?

Only God knows exactly what's in store for you, but He says in His Word that the road to victory begins with a hope and a future and that it is filled with things to prosper you and not to harm you *(Jeremiah 29:11)*.

As for me, I'm going to keep on going down the road to victory to see what the end holds for me. I'll see you from time to time as we travel down this road, won't I?

My Prayer For You

God, I thank you for this journey down the road of victorious living. I thank you for the blessings and the healing that my sister and I have experienced while on this road. I pray that you will seal everything that you have done in our lives and keep us on the path that you have set before us. I pray that my sister will continue to join me on the road to victorious living even as we come to the end of this book. I pray that the lessons and inspirations that she has received will stay with her as she engages in spiritual battles in her everyday life. Help her to know that ultimately the battle is not hers but that you will fight for her if she will just offer it all to you in prayer.

I thank you for the Victory Points that you have imparted to my sister through me and I pray that she will observe each and every one of them, putting them into action in her own life. I thank you for the growth in my sister's life and I thank you for the victory that we have in Jesus.

I ask that you will keep my sister and strengthen her for the remainder of her journey. Let her know that your presence will always be with her and help her to remember that she is with Jesus whenever the crowd or her circumstances try to convince her to quit.

We thank you and we praise you in the name of Jesus. Amen.

A WORD FROM THE LORD

I am with you. Keep your eyes on me. Seek my Kingdom and its righteousness first. Everything else that you need will be provided. Walk with me and talk with me daily. Even when you can't feel my presence, know that I am with you. When you grow weary, I will strengthen you. When you are too tired to go on, I will carry you. As you draw nearer to me, I will keep you safe and I will prosper you. I will guide you through my Word. Mediate on my Word daily and then listen as I speak to you. Never give up. You are more than a conqueror.

♥ Chapter 15

Our Destination – Victorious Living!

If God be for us who can be against us? Who shall separate us from the love of Christ? Shall trouble or hardship or persecution or famine or nakedness or danger or sword? No, in all these things we are more than conquerors through him who loved us.
Romans 8:31,35,37

Well, my friend, we've reached the end of this book but it's not the end of the journey. I know that it's been sad at times, exhilarating at others, and refreshing and cleansing at others.

I pray that you've found healing and hope between the pages of this book. As a matter of fact, I am confident that you received healing and that you have made the shift from living a life of anguish and strife to victorious living because God says that His Word will not come back to Him without accomplishing everything that He sent it to do (Isaiah 55:11). You have made up your mind that from this point forward, you're going to have all that God has in store for you.

You are very close to the final destination that we started out for at the beginning of this book. You have reached the bend in the road called 'Victorious Living' and have made the decision to travel on that road from now on.

Hallelujah! I am praising the Lord just knowing that you have gotten the victory in your life.

Undoubtedly, you will have some opposition as you travel, but be encouraged, because your Father in heaven has already defeated any enemy that will come against you.

I encourage you to keep pressing forward to fulfill God's purpose of victorious living for your life. So in closing, I say, **"Go on my beautiful, Spirit-filled sister and live the victorious life!"**

God bless you!

Let Us Pray Together

Lord God, we come humbly before you thanking you for this journey. We thank you for taking the time to put together such a book so that we can be reminded that we were born for victorious living. Thank you for the testimony that has been shared and thank you for the healing that has taken place in our lives.

We thank you that you have heard the cry of our hearts, that you have seen our secret pain, that you knew that we were broken, busted and disgusted, that you saw it when we were dropped, that you took away the desire for drugs and alcohol, that you showed us real love when we were looking for love in all of the wrong places, that you saw our pain in the midnight hour, that you had a drink of water for us when we were thirsty, that you had a better way for us when we were sick and tired of being sick and tired, that you provided a ray of light in the darkness, that you helped us to stand when we felt like falling, that you helped us to forgive others and to love ourselves, and that you showed us that we didn't have to live broken lives by putting us on the road to victory and staying with us until we reached the destination of victorious living.

Thank you that even though we have learned how to live the victorious life, you will always be with us. So we take the time right now to say, thank you Lord God for caring enough about us to not leave us in the state that we were in. We love you and we cherish you. Amen.

A WORD FROM THE LORD

You are a blessed woman of God. I have made a new covenant with you. I have put my laws in your mind and I have written them on your heart. I am God your Father. You are my daughter. I forgive you of all of the sins that you have committed. I have cast your sins into the sea of forgetfulness. I am the vine of life. Stay connected to me and you will live. Not only will you live, buy also you will live victoriously. I have a great plan for you. In me, you will live and not die. In me you will prosper and not lack. In me, you have the victory.

A Final Note from the Author

Thank you for taking this journey with me. Now that you have been strengthened, it is God's will that you go and minister to another sister or even a brother that you know who may be struggling with some of the issues that I have covered in this book.

"Satan has asked to sift you as wheat. But I have prayed for you, that your faith may not fail. And when you have turned back, strengthen your brothers (and your sisters)." **Luke 22:31**

Please use the prayers in this book to pray for the women (and the men) in your life as well as those who cross your path.

You can help this ministry by putting a copy of this book into the hands of every woman that you know so that their faith may increase and their healing may be made manifest.

May the Lord bless you and keep you eternally.

Sister Rebecca Simmons

About the Author

Who is Rebecca Simmons?

Rebecca Simmons is a woman after God's own heart. She was saved from a life of destruction and unhappiness in 1994 and she has known since then that God had a better plan for her life. She also realized that the trouble and heartache that she had been through in her own life was not for nothing. Later in her Christian walk, she learned that her experiences would be used to help other women to realize that they too can overcome the pain of their pasts and walk the path of victorious living.

Rebecca is married with four children and four grandchildren. She is a Proverbs 31 wife and mother and she and her husband and children live in New Jersey, the state that Rebecca calls home although she was born in Florida. This is credited to the fact that she has lived in Jersey for as long as she can remember.

Rebecca is a Certified Christian Counselor and is a member of the American Association of Christian Counselors. She is a member of the Cathedral International in Perth Amboy, New Jersey where Jesus Christ is Lord and Bishop Donald Hilliard Jr. is the Senior Pastor and her spiritual covering. She acknowledges that she has been called by God to minister to the hurting, the discouraged and those individuals who are seeking "a better way."

Other Works of The Lord Through Rebecca

The Lord has also led Rebecca to write another inspirational book entitled *Man Problems*. This book addresses the issues of Molestation, Abandonment and Neglect by the fathers and the men in the lives of women everywhere. Under God's divine guidance, she has written two healing novels, *Nobody's Business* and *Daddy Love*. Both of these novels take a realistic look at relationships through the lives of fictional characters that women and men across America find themselves relating to. She has also co-written, *Kayla's Day*, a children's motivational book, with her six-year-old daughter, Kayla. This book deposits basic lessons of motivation and determination into the hearts of children while they are still young. Thereby when they are old they will not stray away from these teachings.

Rebecca is also a prolific speaker who breaks the bread of wisdom concerning all aspects of life and relationships in a caring but no-nonsense manner.

Resources for Help

National Domestic Violence Hotline
www.NDVH.org
1-800-799-7233

RAINN
Rape, Abuse and Incest
National Network
www.rainn.org

National Sexual Assault Hotline
1-800-656-HOPE
24 hours/confidential

New Life Ministries
www.Newlife.com
1-800-639-5433

Alcoholics Anonymous
www.alcoholics-anonymous.org

Narcotics Anonymous
www.na.org

The Cry Of A Woman's Heart
Order Form
Use this convenient order form to order additional
Copies of
The Cry Of A Woman's Heart

Please Print:

Name: _____

Address: _____

City: _____ **State:** _____

Zip Code: _____

Phone: (   ) _____

_____ Copies of book @ $12.95 each $ _____
Postage and handling @ $2.50 per book $ _____
NJ residents add .78 tax per book $ _____
Total amount enclosed $ _____

Make checks payable to
Diligence Publishing Company

Send to Diligence Publishing Company
41 Watchung Plaza #239
Montclair, NJ 07042

Visit the author's website at
www.NewLifeSpeakers.com or
Visit the publisher's site at www.DPC-Books.Com
Phone: 973-680-8438